DISMANTLING FAMILY COURT CORRUPTION

Why Taking
The Kids
Was Not
Enough

Maryann Petri

Disclaimer:

The names and dates in this book have been changed
to protect the anonymity of those in this story, but all of
it are actual events.

Copyright © 2020 by Maryann Petri. All rights reserved.
ISBN 978-1-64871-836-6
Dismantling Family Court Corruption:
Why Taking The Kids Wasn't Enough
www.DismantlingFamilyCourtCorruption.com
MaryannPetri3@gmail.com
published by **Triumph Press**

10 9 8 7 6 5 4 3 2 1

Acknowledgements

This book is dedicated to my husband, Brad, for his constant strength, encouragement and support during these dark years.

I thank Tina Craig for her support and many years of dedicated friendship, and Linda McIntire for her constant support as well as Carolyn Pershing for her understanding and support.

I would like to thank Dr. Fredrick Bond and Jen Larson, L.C.S.W. for all their specialized support and input.

I thank my Dad, my Blessing, for getting me through all my legal matters, seeing me through this grueling process and, ultimately, saving my life.

My main motivation for writing this book is to support those who have endured such emotional duress that they have lost their way of life, belief system, livelihood, and sanity; those who have committed suicide in the midst of seeing their broken children taken away while losing their fight against a corrupt and maniacal Family Court System.

Contents

Introduction

The events that took place over a number of years in this story need to be heard. I wrote this book to help others conquer their fears and the pain caused by Family Court in the form of Parental Alienation. In telling this story, the reader should be aware of the depravity that dwells behind the closed doors within the Family Courtroom. Bias, collusion and perjury link themselves like a chain that is weighted down by an anchor known as corruption. Surviving the Family Court system requires all resources and abilities.

There may come a time when going Pro Se is your only choice to fight not only for yourself, but for your family. The decision to go this route usually happens when you become financially drained. At the Pro Se level, you are on your own; no one to catch you or comfort you when opposing counsel demeans you in a courtroom in front of everyone. The judge sits back and says nothing. Radio silence. But a show of confidence will keep you grounded as you stand firm and display all the lies and deception to the judge. As a Pro Se goes along, you begin to learn from the opponents, their documents and judge's orders. These will be the guides to help prove success even when you think you are failing. Failing will happen, but there will be small successes and then major victories...

Pushing forward with perseverance, never stopping and never giving up, is the linchpin of success through such trials. You may think you are not winning or are ever going to win but in the end success comes in many forms.

PART ONE
Background

The Writing On The Wall

The first 15 months of my marriage and the courtship with my ex-husband were wonderful. After that, it slowly devolved into a living nightmare. We first met after a friend set me up on a blind date with Seth Balor. We became fast friends and fell in love very quickly, riding our bikes along the pond and going to practically every movie that came out.

Looking back, I can see red flags in my courtship, but I was blind to them at the time. From the beginning, Seth treated me with disrespect. For instance, we once went to a concert and got lost in traffic. When I suggested a different way home, he exploded and yelled at me. I justified his behavior, thinking that he was stressed, but this was more than just a one-time incident. For my bridal shower, I bought a nice dress for $75.00 at a department store. I planned a lot of use for it in the future. I was excited to show him the dress, but when I did, he showed utter disappointment. He couldn't believe I had spent so much money on it. Instead of being happy on that special day, sadness loomed throughout the festivities.

Prior to going to the church for my rehearsal dinner, one of my bridesmaids took me out to a local bar during Happy Hour. A man bought me a beer to celebrate my marriage, and I drank less than half of it before leaving for the rehearsal. As soon as we got to the church, Seth came up to me and said, "I smell alcohol on your breath. I don't want anyone smelling that! I'm not marrying you tomorrow if you have alcohol on your breath." He did not want to hear what had actually happened, and I barely spoke to Seth for the rest of the evening because I was so upset. I couldn't wait to leave the rehearsal dinner, get home, and rest.

Later that evening, around 10:00 p.m., Seth called and apologized for his behavior. He told me to forget it had happened. I should've called the wedding off at that very moment. Instead, I justified his behavior again, telling myself that it was just the pre-wedding jitters.

The wedding was beautiful, but it was the hottest day on record. Looking back, I consider it a bad omen, because the next ten years of my life would turn into a living hell.

Sweden

As the years passed, our relationship became more tense. One evening, I found a credit card statement with a $3,500 expenditure on it that I knew nothing about. I was furious. At this point, Seth had already yelled at me in intervals over the course of our relationship, and I was afraid to confront him directly, so I wrote Seth a letter that night expressing my anger and concerns. The following day, he read the letter and shouted at me, asking me why I didn't want to talk to him about it in person.

A year passed, and I had slowly saved $5,000.00 in a high interest money-market account to surprise Seth at Christmastime as he wanted to move out of our apartment. When I surprised him with this gift on Christmas Day, he did not appreciate it. Seth shouted, "Why were you hiding this money from me? We needed this money! All I did was worry about paying the bills!" He never had trouble making payments or seemed anxious about paying the bills before. When he realized that there would be enough money to buy a fixer upper due to this savings, however, Seth was finally a little grateful for it.

Seth was also disrespectful to my parents and family members. After moving in, my parents came over to see us. They were worried about me driving 20 miles each day to the psychiatric unit where I worked as a registered nurse, so my father bought me a cell phone and offered to make the monthly payments on it. As soon as Seth saw this, he shouted at my father that it wasn't his responsibility or business to do that. My father left the phone with me and walked out of our home with tears in his eyes. Seth never apologized for how he treated him.

There were times things were running smoothly, depending on Seth's mood. Even after having our first baby, a sweet little girl, sometimes he would become moody. My life became even more isolated, especially with having a newborn in tow and especially when Seth was offered a job opportunity in Sweden to further his career. A new company wanted us to move to Stockholm so Seth could be trained by a top Swedish company that specialized in computer software. In time, he would open a company in the United States. At the time, the idea excited me, and I didn't mind giving up my career for a while to support him. While there, his mood changed into a rollercoaster.

Soon, even my days with Seth became contentious. In the months that followed, we stayed at his mother's house while we waited for our Green Card to come through. One night, Seth and I went out to watch a movie. Afterwards, I brought up some concerns. The conversation escalated so severely that I told him I wasn't going to move to Sweden with him. We drove back to his parent's house and stood in their driveway, still arguing. He begged me to go with him. "Can we put this behind us?" he repeated again and again. Oh how I wish that I had decided not to go with him!

We flew into the Stockholm, Arlanda Airport, and traveled to our new home in Stockholm. The company-provided home was an elegant ranch-style house with a small kitchen, a living room with a fireplace and a dining room leading to an enclosed sun porch. The house had four furnished bedrooms. The backyard garden had extravagant brickwork for a pathway and foliage. Every weekend, we drove around, looking at ancient castles and shops.

But despite the beauty around us, things were not going as smoothly as I hoped. Our relationship was becoming increasingly fragile. When Seth returned home from work, he sat in his chair and watched the news. Then he would take a long bath, go to bed, and essentially ignore me and our daughter. When he did talk to us, he had mood swings that made it stressful and unpredictable to be around him.

By our second year in Sweden, my lack of friendships and support was wearing on me. I had been friends with a woman during my first year there, but she had found a full-time job and was now unavailable. So I stayed busy taking our baby out to stores nearby. Then, I went home to watch TV while she fell asleep on my lap.

During that time, I wanted my daughter to have a baby brother or sister so she would not end up as an only child. Months and months passed with no results. My depression deepened, and I was soon unable to sleep, waking every night at 2:00 a.m. When I tried to talk to Seth about my concerns and growing depression, he didn't want anything to do with it. He said that he had enough on his plate already.

I started praying for a child, and I saw a family physician to help with my anxiety. My Mother-In-Law was praying, too. I learned how to crochet and made a baptismal bonnet for the new baby, even though I wasn't even pregnant yet. I saw it as an act of faith in God that He would provide.

In May, my daughter and I were at home watching the movie, "The Coneheads." I decided to take a pregnancy test, as I was running a little late on my cycle. Like so many others, this test was negative. Disappointed, I threw the test in the trash can. Longing for a positive result, I pulled it back out of the trash can after about three hours. The test was positive! I couldn't believe it. I remember yelling and laughing, "Praise the Lord and pass the ammunition!" I called Seth at work, and when he answered the phone I announced, "Beldar, I am with Cone." He laughed and said, "Congratulations!" Both of us were laughing and happy.

Seth and I still traveled around Sweden, visiting castles and cafes, but my new pregnancy made even these small things exhausting. When I told Seth that I couldn't walk up the steep steps of one of the castles with a two-year old in tow, he became angry. He told me I was being selfish, and we drove home in silence. At one point he became so angered during a disagreement he raised a knife to me; however I was not afraid because I just thought he was trying to scare me.

We flew back permanently to the United States in early Fall. At the time, I was struggling with morning sickness, so Seth suggested we sit in the back of the plane. Unfortunately, there was a lot of turbulence, and that made my nausea worse. As soon as we landed and made it through customs, I bolted for the bathroom and vomited.

Returning to the U.S.

When we returned home, we stayed at his mother's house while we waited for the renters in our home to leave. Unfortunately, that did not do any favors for our marriage. Everything had to be done his mother's way — from leaving pot handles out over the edge of the stove where my daughter could reach them to insisting that my daughter eat more when she was already full. The relationship I had with my mother-in-law changed dramatically and it was as if we were in her way at all times. Seth agreed, and we finally decided to move out. Even though our home desperately needed remodeling, we didn't care.

After we returning to the U.S., I went into labor with my second child. I was sitting on the sofa awaiting instructions from my physician.. When I told Seth that I was going into labor, he knew he would have to take the day off, looked disgruntled and asked in disbelief, "What are we going to do for money?" I looked up at him with shock on my face.

I delivered a sweet baby boy later that afternoon. The midwife said my son was the fastest delivery she ever saw. He was born with big, blue eyes— the eyes of an old soul, she said. My baby boy came into the world fast that I thought he would be born on the roadside in the snow. As soon as his sister, who was wearing her pink "Big Sister" shirt, saw him, she walked over and said, "You're cute," then ran to my bed, jumped in my arms, and sat on my lap.

Several months later, I conceived my last baby, which I soon discovered were twins. My two boys were born that following August, both with full heads of hair.

Returning to Work

A couple months after the twins were born, Seth continuously told me every day after coming home from work that he was worried he would lose his job. It was scaring me that this could happen, so I went back to being a nurse in case anything should take place.

While I was nervous about going back into nursing, my preceptor did a great job easing me into the medical field. She guided me back to the med-surgical aspect and taught me about all the new updated equipment and how to handle patients that came out of surgery. I ended up absolutely loving it. Nursing gave me purpose and helped me cope with the stress at home.

I soon became friends with Linda McIntire, who would transport patients up to the floors several times a shift. She would be a great friend and support to me after my husband and I divorced. When Linda got to know me, she gave me the nickname, "Pippy." At that time, I wore my hair in two ponytails and put my pens in the ponytail so I wouldn't lose them. Apparently, everyone thought that was cute. I loved helping patients navigate through their fears of an unknown illness and learning complex medications. Every day was a new experience.

One day I was watching a talk show, and they were discussing personality disorders. When I worked on the psychiatric unit, this wasn't addressed in-depth as we dealt with very sick patients with Schizophrenia and Bipolar Disorder. This fascinated me and the speaker said to avoid them at all costs. But then I got to thinking long and hard. I was living with a personality disorder. I was already at the point of being out of love and wanted nothing to do with him and the mood swings. I had gotten fed up and knew it was time.

Picture from Nursing School Graduation

After the Divorce

When I told Seth I wanted a divorce, I didn't believe it would bother him. We hadn't been happy or connected for a long time, and our relationship was completely devoid of love. Oh, how wrong I was. The day after I told Seth I wanted a divorce, he began using mind games on my daughter. He told me that he was going to tell her I was the reason this divorce was happening. What kind of person tells that to a six year old? I wish I would have known this would be the beginning of him brainwashing her. I quickly shot back that if he told her that, I would tell her that he drove me to it.

For a while things were pretty normal. We came to our own agreement and stayed out of the court system. We had 50/50 custody and seemed to get along okay, if only for the sake of the kids. I found an old, beautiful house built in 1900 to live in, and Seth inspected it for me. His house was close to mine, which would work well with our new co-parenting arrangements. We had a verbal agreement that he would help me put in a new kitchen and bathroom, and install insulation in the crawl space above the four bedrooms. What I didn't know, however, was that he intentionally stepped on the air ducts that heated all four of our bedrooms. Years later when I went to sell the house, I was told I needed a small second furnace for the upstairs bedroom. The man that installed it looked around in the attic and explained to me all the ducts had been smashed flat. He said he would have to replace them and that would increase the cost by well over $800.00. I knew Seth had done this on purpose. But why? The children needed to be kept warm. How could he step on much-needed ducts that would keep his children warm?

Whenever I struggled to discipline my kids, Seth was there to help. Sometimes you need a strong male voice to get the point across. I didn't call Seth all the time, just here and there when

I needed him, such as when my oldest boy was picking on his younger siblings. My children came first and work came second, so my schedule was always put around whatever the kids were doing. My daughter, for example, was a talented singer, so I regularly taxied her to music lessons and rehearsals for school plays. I also ran them to dental appointments and took them to the family doctor when they were sick.

During the Summer, I took the kids to the pool twice a day. We swam from 1-5 p.m., went home for macaroni and cheese or Happy Meals, and returned to the pool from 6-8 p.m. After the pool, we would head home and get ready for bed. I allowed them to watch T.V. until 9:00 p.m. and then the lights were off. Sometimes we all sat in my bed together and watched a movie until we fell asleep. It wasn't until one evening, when my youngest son told me, "I feel like dad doesn't take care of me." that I began to worry that something was wrong.

📖 TAKEAWAY:

I believe it is a good idea to study several personality disorders. Narcissistic Personality Disorder, Borderline Personality Disorder and Bipolar Disorder. A young person needs to study these in-depth so when they get into a relationship and see these behaviors, they can leave before becoming deeply involved.

Building Our Separate Lives

Blind Date with Judith

Seth was feeling depressed. He knew I was starting to see other people, and he was having a hard time accepting that. He often asked if I knew any nurses that might be interested in dating him. Then, one day, he called me while intoxicated and told me he was considering committing suicide. I was horrified. I urged him not to make this mistake and promised things would be better soon. I told him I would keep an eye out for someone he could date, hoping this would calm him down. I even sent books that I thought would cheer him up. There wasn't any more talk of suicide after that.

Several years later, I set Seth up with Judith, an acquaintance of ours who had been recently divorced. Apparently, Judith called Seth on his birthday and they talked for several hours. Within two weeks, she moved in with him. Soon, they set a wedding date for eight months in the future. To this day, I regret setting my husband up with that woman. But how could I know what a nightmare she, in conjunction with Seth, would become to our family?

The Wedding

Worried that my husband's new relationship was moving too quickly, I asked him about a Pre-Nuptial Agreement, as I believed this would be in the best interest of our children. He told me he wouldn't do that, saying, "She'll take my money anyway," in a sad, hopeless tone.

Seth and Judith planned a wedding on the water, by a small, elegant pond near the wetlands. Then, Judith and Seth took a three-week honeymoon to Aruba. When the kids came over to visit, they showed me pictures of their father's wedding. The boys had blue shirts on and my daughter was wearing a pink, flowered dress that had ruffles on the shoulder straps. Judith and Seth stood together with our children around them. None of my children were smiling. I also noticed that a judge was officiating the ceremony.

I was optimistic about the situation. Judith was the same religion as me, and I was hopeful she would help get my kids to Sunday school and maybe even to church on the weekends when I didn't have them. Sadly, I was gravely mistaken about how this relationship would work.

The First of Many Threats

A month after the wedding, Judith and I talked on the phone about the children. Suddenly, the conversation turned South, "You know I work in the courthouse, right?" she asked.

"Yes, I guess so," I said, not sure why Judith would bring this up.

"And I know police officers too; I know a lot of the policemen at the police station."

I didn't respond and quickly changed the subject. Were these veiled threats? I couldn't believe Judith would actually threaten me like that for no reason at all, so I quickly brushed the worries out of my mind.

This wasn't the last time Judith would threaten me. On a rainy October day, I asked Seth to return some flowerpots. I was home alone, and the children were in school. I thought he would just leave them on the porch, but instead there was intense pounding on my front door and upon opening it, there stood Seth and Judith. We exchanged words briefly. At that point, Judith stepped forward and spoke to me in a low, demeaning tone, "I know a lot of people at the courthouse, and I'm friends with all the judges," she reminded me. I yelled something back at her while slamming the door. I could actually feel the house shake as the door slammed shut.

I was never invited inside Seth and Judith's home, so I didn't have much context about what life was like there for my kids. During one phone call, however, I learned that it was anything but harmonious. On that day, I called my ex-husband to discuss a disciplinary issue I was having with one of the kids. When Seth answered the phone, Judith was screaming in the background. Seth shouted back in unison and soon the yelling was so chaotic, I had to hang up. Months later, I called again because I believed one of my sons needed to see a counselor. Again, when Seth picked up the phone there was intense yelling and screaming from both Seth and Judith. He shouted, "The problems are all with you! You need help!" and hung up. Our co-parenting relationship was broken. I never called him back again.

Finding the Love of My Life

Several years passed, and I continued to date, searching for someone who would be worthy of our family. The men I dated were decent people, but they were all unable to commit. Even when I was exhausted from all of my failed relationships, I refused to stop dating. My mother was deeply religious, and when I went through the divorce she was adamantly against it. One day, she stood in the kitchen while my three children ran around the house and screamed, "No one is going to want you and your three kids!" I was determined to prove her wrong.

One evening, during a slow night at work, I went into an empty patient room and pulled out a copy of the Bible. Then I took it back to the nurse's station and read Mark 11:22-24, where Jesus says, "Have faith in God...whoever say unto this mountain, 'Be lifted up and thrown into the sea and does not doubt in his heart but believes that what he says will happen, it shall be done for him. Therefore I tell you, all that you ask for in prayer, believe that you will receive it and it shall be yours." These verses gave me the strength to keep searching for my husband.

I messaged my future husband at the end of July on a dating site. We exchanged phone numbers and started talking. He was an independent contractor traveling around the country and outside of the U.S. on various projects. At the time I met Brad, he was on unemployment. This would happen from time to time in his line of work, but in this case it actually worked in our favor; it gave us the whole summer to date and get to know each other without interruptions.

We met the first week of July at a small diner in town. As soon as I sat down, Brad showed me a picture of his sister, who had a toddler standing beside her. I smiled and said, "That's Joy!" Though I had never met Brad, I had been friends with his sister for 15 years. This felt like a good omen to me. We talked for a couple hours, and upon leaving, we agreed to meet again for a motorcycle ride.

On our next date, Brad picked me up on his BMW motorcycle, and we met up with some of his friends. That evening, I took him aside and said I was searching for a second husband who could fully commit to me and my children. Brad held my hands, looked into my eyes, and promised me that he was looking for the same thing.

As we continued dating, Brad re-introduced me to his sister, Joy. She and I would make dinner together or meet up at the pool with our kids and soon became close friends. Her husband, Philip, would come over after work and join us. I was overjoyed. I had always wanted a large family, and now I finally felt like I had one!

The months rolled on, and Joy and I would go to the mall to buy clothing and things for our children, stopping at our favorite coffee shop. We dubbed it, "Days of Joy." We had a good laugh over that as we planned the next "Day of Joy."

Eventually, I got to meet Brad's whole family, including his two brothers. His mother was a wonderful woman. She suffered with severe rheumatoid arthritis and used a wheelchair because of how crippled her body had become from it. She also had a back surgery that went badly a few years previous. Nonetheless, she was a bright and positive person. She liked me right away, and I have to admit that she would be the kindest mother-in-law I would ever know. His father was very personable, himself a retired contractor, and a jovial character to be around. The both of them readily accepted my children as their own grandchildren, and they were as happy to have us as I was to have them.

Preparing for Marriage

Brad and I began looking at engagement rings in early September. At 44, this was Brad's first marriage. We took the kids with us to the jewelers, along with his niece and nephew. It was such a fun evening! When we left the store and got into his truck, his niece announced to me, "My uncle is expensive." I totally laughed. How true that statement proved to be.

After we were engaged, Brad took a job out of town. I wouldn't be able to see him for several months, but we spoke on the phone every day. That was the nature of his job, but I didn't mind spending time alone. After all, I had already done that for many years.

In the meantime, Joy planned our wedding. She, my daughter and I went out to pick bridesmaid dresses. I let my daughter pick them and, she did a wonderful job finding the perfect, most flattering dresses.

At the kid's request, I moved into Brad's house six months earlier, as it was nicer than mine. Brad's basement was converted into a movie theater complete with a silver screen, computerized movie access, surround sound speakers and recliners and sofas. So, as you can imagine, the kids absolutely loved it there. Once we were settled into our new marriage, I put my house on the market.

We set the date for the end of Fall and got married at the largest church in town with an elaborate reception. It was a warm, sunny day. We were all dancing, even my children. I have a lovely photo of us all hugging each other at once. My daughter didn't want to leave early, and I reassured her that we would all stay until it was completely finished. That day couldn't have been more wonderful.

The wedding day was wonderful!

Once it was over, I hugged my children goodbye in the parking lot so that Brad and I could head to our one-week honeymoon. My parents took the kids back to their apartment so they could change out of the wedding clothes, and their father picked them up from there.

When I got into our car the next day to head to our destination, my daughter called. "Mom, I need to talk to you," she said in between sobs, "Judith and I got in a fight, and it's just so terrible. I need you!" I remember this as if it happened yesterday; they had argued about the wedding itself and the dresses she picked out.

I didn't know what to do. Should I take her and all the other kids with us on our honeymoon? I wanted to do that, but I worried that it wouldn't be fair to Brad. Instead, my daughter and I talked for almost an hour. Once she had calmed down, I hung up and Brad and I headed to our destination. To this day, I wish I could take that choice back. I should've never left her alone in such an awful situation.

I finally had everything I wanted: an extended family, a loving husband, and a good relationship with my children. But little did I know that my entire life was only moments away from falling apart. That following September, Seth filed for a Modification of the Child Support.

My attorney told me I didn't need to go to the Child Support Conference, but looking back on what happened, I really wish I had. During the conference, it was concluded that Seth was allegedly making about as much money as I was, so my child support was discontinued. My attorney called from the hallway, out of ear-shot, and explained this to me. I couldn't believe it; there was no way this was true! He stated, "Maybe they are cheap with him. He seems like a nice guy." I replied, "If he was such a nice guy, then why did I divorce him?" I began to look for another attorney.

I was stunned. How could my attorney say that after Seth had just taken everything away from me like that? How was I even going to survive? I needed that child support to pay the bills, the mortgage, and my car payment!

I desperately needed to sell my home — and quickly! It was the only way I would ever be able to take care of my own needs, but it had already been sitting on the market for one year. Panicked, I called my parents and told them what had happened.

The next day, my father told me he would cover my mortgage until the house sold. I was so relieved and grateful. If it wasn't for his help, I don't know what would have happened to my credit. Grateful for the extra time, I called a new realtor to see if she could help. She came and visited the home, but the only suggestion she had was to paint the kitchen a different color. It wasn't much, but it was better than nothing, so I did it as quickly as I could.

By that Monday, a buyer wanted to see the house. I tried not to get my hopes up. I didn't hear anything until Thursday when the realtor called. "Good news," the realtor said over the phone, "They want the house, congratulations!"

What a miracle! We closed at the end of the year. I offered to pay my father back for the mortgage he had covered, but he refused to take even a cent. Brad sold his home as well, and we were able to purchase a larger, nicer home where each of my kids were able to have their own bedrooms.

The First Hearing

In the early Spring, I met with a new attorney to discuss the child support situation, and we filed another modification. Then, that April, my attorney and I went before the Honorable Judge Margerita Speer for a De Novo Hearing. De Novo is the Latin phrase for new beginning— far from it. I don't know who came up with that title, but the only beginning this was for me was the beginning of endless nightmares and a rapid weight loss that soon followed.

"Look to your left," I told my attorney while we were waiting for the judge to appear, "The most beautiful woman in the world is sitting right over there." My attorney chuckled. There Judith sat, front and center in the pew, leaning over with her elbows on her knees, eyes wide with excitement. She must have taken a break to be there.

Emma Black, my husband's attorney, paused in the middle of her sentences which made me think she was asking questions, so I would answer. Then, Attorney Black would continue to talk and the judge began scolding me for interrupting! The whole thing was ridiculous. This must have occurred six times. When it was over, my ex-husband went over to Attorney Black and Judith; they smiled and laughed together as if they were close friends!

When we left the courtroom, my attorney was as disgusted as I was and said, "I don't understand the way she's been ruling these days." **Several weeks later, the judge's orders were sent in the mail. Judge Speer awarded me $250.00 per month for my four children. It was a slap in the face compared to what I actually needed.**

 **TAKEAWAY:**

Go with your gut. If you think your children need you in a time of crisis, and you are allowed access to them, take them. Learn when an attorney is baiting you, this is an old tactic that I wish my current attorney would have told me about. If a third party individual is involved in a courthouse where your case is, report to their boss any inappropriate comments. If anything happens in the hallways of the courthouse, anything out of the ordinary, go up to the Sherriff's office and have them pull the footage.

PART TWO:
The Betrayal

You Can't Go

"Make no mistake what happens when Parental Alienation occurs. A child, who may previously have had a perfectly normal and loving relationship with both parents, is put in the position of being forced to choose one and reject the other, often through manipulation. When parental alienation occurs, adults are often deceiving their children to reject and even hate the parent they love. From many different angles, almost any angle you approach it, the family court system seems broken, biased and should be thoroughly investigated. This massive, multi-billion industry must be examined."

— Julio Rivera, Townhall

Grooming

Seth and Judith began brainwashing my daughter around the age of eight years old. They engaged in a type of emotional abuse known as Parental Alienation, which is a tactic that dysfunctional parents use to get their children to hate or even abandon the other parent. Though I never saw the abuse, aside from hearing shouting over the phone or what my children shared with me, I could see the signs of it in my son and daughter's behavior.

Parental Alienation is the process and the result of psychological manipulation of a child into showing unwarranted fear, disrespect or hostility towards a parent and/or other family members. It is a distinctive form of psychological abuse that occurs almost exclusively in association with family separation or divorce, particularly where legal action is involved. It often leads to the long-term or even permanent estrangement of a child from one parent and other family members and, as a particularly adverse childhood experience, results in significantly increased lifetime risks of both mental and physical illness.

Mr. Stephen Best, psychotherapist of the United Kingdom, states, "Parental Alienation is one of the most insidious forms of child emotional and psychological abuse. The deliberate manipulation of your own children to make them not only hate but often fear their other parent is absolutely abhorrent. Children live with the effects of alienation for the rest of their lives, and it damages their chances of reaching their full potential. Often, alienated children become involved in crime and a disproportional number of children growing up without access to one of their parents end up serving time in prison. Alienated children are also less likely to achieve in education and often suffer from depression. If a child is being physically or sexually abused, would people turn a blind eye and ignore it? Well Parental Alienation is just as damaging as physical or sexual abuse. You can't see the bruises or the scars, but they are there on the inside. Don't look the other way, speak out. Many of the general public do not know about Parental Alienation and this needs to change."

Barbara Fidler explained some of the signs of Parental Alienation that include:

- Rejection and denigration of a parent for reasons that are trivial

- Rigid refusal to consider alternative views or explanations

- Repetition of the favored parent's words
- Rehearsed (or it sounds like rehearsed) script
- Relatives are included in the rejection (even pets)
- Little or no regret or guilt regarding behavior towards the parent being rejected.

Over the next few years, my children began to exhibit all of these signs. For example, my daughter used to cuddle in bed with me. Then, one evening, she suddenly jumped out of the bed and walked out, yelling, "I'm too old to sleep with my mother anymore!" Of course, I had no problem with her believing she was too old to sleep in my bed, but how she reacted was cruel and unexpected.

Then she started lying to me. One morning, Joy and her kids stopped by to go with us to school. My children were getting their coats on and the entry way coat rack suddenly fell to the floor. My daughter blamed it on her brothers. We were in a hurry to go to school, so I swept it aside and didn't inquire further. Later, Joy pulled me aside and told me she had seen my daughter knock the coat rack onto the floor.

My daughter was around eight years old, and I took her aside for a heart-to-heart about what happened. All she had to do was tell me the truth. I also explained to her that I wanted to raise nice children, children that weren't mean to others. I told her I overheard her talking poorly about one of her friends, and I didn't want that going on either. She started to cry. What I would later learn about my daughter, after the indications, after all the family court hearings were over with all their lies and financial destruction, was that my daughter had no regard for the feelings of others — even at a young age.

The increased anxiety in my oldest son, beginning around the age seven, was another red flag for me. He would start crying before school started, and when he would get to school, he ended up in the counselor's office wanting me to come talk to him. What I didn't know was where was all this anxiety was coming from and who was causing it. My once-happy son had turned into a basket case.

The twins internalized everything. They were so much like me as a child. They seemed to slip under the radar and were taken for "happy-go-lucky." They held their trauma inside. The twins told me I was being badly talked about in their father's home, yet they remained stoic. Then one day, the three of them just stopped smiling.

No, Mom, You Can't!

On a beautiful Sunday in mid-Fall, my daughter, who was 17 at the time, sang the National Anthem with a pure, strong voice at an event. She sounded beautiful! Afterwards, we all had lunch sitting down at a formal and pretty table with flowers in the centerpiece. As we sat there, waiting for the buffet to start, my daughter said, "I'm going to sing the National Anthem at the new library tomorrow."

"Great, I'll come!" I said, excited to hear my daughter sing again.

"No, Mom, you can't," she said.

"Why not?" I asked.

"You just can't." my daughter said, digging in her heels.

"Why not?" I asked, "It's a public place. Is there somebody that I can call and ask about it? I'd really like to see you!"

My daughter continued to insist that I couldn't go and that she didn't want me to call the library. Finally, after a bit of an argument, I decided to let it be until the morning. When the morning came, I again asked my daughter why I couldn't go to this event. "I told you, it's not open to the public," she said again. The conversation quickly escalated, and she soon started attacking me about all sorts of topics, much of which were completely inappropriate to bring up around her younger siblings. "Stop the verbal abuse!" I shouted, "You have no right to treat your mother like this."

My daughter came back downstairs, now ready for school, dragging a garbage bag full of clothes behind her. At the time, I assumed the clothes were for a singing competition or some other event in her school, as she was involved in a lot of different projects. Soon, she was screaming at me again, "You're ruining my chance of singing in public!" she shouted, "This is a good opportunity, and you're ruining it!"

As we drove to school, I said, "Okay, this just isn't adding up. Libraries are a public place, and I don't believe you're telling me the truth. So since you lied to your mother, I'm not giving you permission to sing at this event. You will just have to go to school instead. After all you just told me last week that you should be in school instead of putting time into singing." My daughter was infuriated.

I dropped my three boys off at the middle school first, and then I drove to my daughter's high school. When we arrived, she stormed out of the car, looking at me briefly before leaving. I wonder what I would have done differently if I had known the next time I would see her was in the hallway of a courthouse.

Later that day, around noon, I received a call from CPS, a Lilith Bean was asking to come over and what would be a good time. I was shocked and told them three o'clock. Thank God Brad was off work, and I jokingly told him to start cleaning the house.

I went to pick up my daughter from the high school and sat at the curb to pick her up. Students flooded through the doors as I looked around, waiting for my daughter to appear. When the flood turned into a trickle, and soon almost no students came out at all,

I knew that she wasn't coming. I figured she must have gone with her father, but I tried not to be too worried about it. *This will all blow over soon* I told myself, *right?* Quickly, I rushed to the middle school to pick up the boys to get back to the house by 3:00.

 TAKEAWAY:

If you are concerned that your children or the children of someone you know may be suffering from Parental Alienation, there are many ways to recognize the signs before they occur. Dr Childress explains what Parental Alienation symptoms are:

1) Attachment System Suppression, which leads the child to cling to one parent and attempt to completely eliminate their relationship with an affectionately available parent.

2) Personality Disorder traits INCLUDING the narcissistic traits of GRANDIOSITY (believing they are above and more important than the rejected parent), AN ABSENCE OF EMPATHY towards the target-reject parent, ENTITLEMENT, (expecting the target-reject parent to give them whatever they want exactly as they want it), A HAUGHTY AND ARROGANT ATTITUDE, and SPLITTING (idealizing the supposedly favored parent over the target-reject parent).

3) In addition, the child will show a PHOBIC FEAR or excessive anxiety towards the target-reject parent, which will eventually become so severe they will try to avoid the loving parent altogether. Eventually, the kids will hold the belief that the target-parent actually is abusive, even when

the target-parent has never done anything outside of the normal range of parenting.

Dr Childress explains, "There is absolutely zero reason why a mental health professional should not, at the very least, assess for the presence or absence of these three symptom features in the child's symptom display. If the child does not display these symptoms and these symptoms are not present then there is nothing to worry about. If, however these three symptoms are present in the child's symptom display, then the...diagnosis is... Child Psychological Abuse, Confirmed. This is an issue of child protection. This is simple. This is direct. This is straightforward."

"Some of the stories are heartbreaking," says Barbara Fidler, Clinical-Developmental Psychologist in Toronto who specializes in high-conflict parenting. She says her caseload is growing. "I actually lose sleep over these families. We are losing sleep because children are suffering."

Fidler is working on a special issue of the Family Court Review due early 2020 with Queens University Law professor, Nick Bala. They hope the collection of all the latest data on Parental Alienation will inform family lawyers, judges and therapists around the world.

"This is clearly a big problem," says Bala. "I get emails from people coast, to coast and internationally, raising concerns about being cut off from their children, being cut off from grandchildren."

A growing body of research is illuminating the effects of Parental Alienation on children, says Fidler, including:

- Self-hatred and self-esteem issues
- Higher rates and risks of depression, relationship difficulties and substance abuse.
- Loss of guidance and support of one parent

- Loss of relationship with extended family
- Inability to develop and sustain healthy relationships

Fidler and Bala say there is a need for more research into how to better define alienation in its various forms, since not all cases look the same. "It's not just a mental health issue, but a legal issue that should require better training for family lawyers and judges, who can put a stop to alienation early."

"We need to recognize the problem earlier so that we can provide the education and in some cases therapy early on," says Fidler.

A CPS Nightmare

"The violence and judicial abuse in family courts would not be possible without the support [corruption] of the Department of Children and Families [CPS]"

- Keith Harmon Snow

When Lilith arrived, she was alone. I knew that it was in my best interest to be kind to CPS workers, so I smiled when I opened the door and said, "Come in! Can I offer you something to drink?" Inside, my parents were sitting down in the living room getting ready for family dinner.

"Yes, very nice." Lilith said, looking around. "I'd like to speak with you in private; if you can arrange that."

My parents offered to take the twins, who were upstairs in their rooms, outside to go to the park. When they were gone, Lilith looked around our home and in the kid's bedrooms. Then, we both sat down on the sofa. Brad sat in the chair opposite of us.

Before Lilith even sat down, she said, "If these indications of emotional abuse are founded in regards to your daughter, you will lose your job as a registered nurse."

"I'm sorry, what?" I asked in disbelief, "Emotional abuse? What are you talking about?"

Lilith belittled me, telling me that it was my fault that my daughter was gone and accusing me of all sorts of things I had never done. "Do you know where your daughter is?! Do you know where your daughter is?!" she shouted. At this point, Brad was extremely upset, but Lilith wouldn't allow him to get a single word in to disagree with her.

"Could you keep it down?" I asked. My oldest son was in the next room, playing his X-box, and I didn't want him to hear this awful conversation.

Lilith paid me no mind. "Do you love your kids more than you hate your ex?" she yelled at me. "Do you love your kids more than you hate your ex?"

I was so confused and overwhelmed that I struggled to even understand Lilith's questions. I had never been treated so terribly before, not even as a nurse by other patients! I was terrified that my children could be taken away. "Stop talking to me like that; I'm a nurse!" I yelled. I told her that I wasn't stupid or a drug abuser, as she had accused me of being emotionally abusive toward my child.

Lilith Bean then asked about the child support monies and why I was not happy with the amount I was being paid. I told her I was getting $250.00 per month for the total of four children, and it simply wasn't enough for me to care for their needs. Lilith Bean stated that I should be happy with what the court deemed appropriate. Instead of discussing my daughter and the reasons why she left home, she hammered on child support again and again.

Lilith also accused me of "bad-mouthing the father" mentioning a sign I had put in my vehicle almost two years ago that, according to her, said "Seth is a dead-beat dad."

I couldn't believe this sign was being brought up again! It had only been on my car for three days, and I hadn't heard the end of it from my ex-husband since. The sign had said, "Strong guys pay child support and some don't care." It had already been addressed in court and with our co-parenting counselor, who had to tell Seth to stop harping about it because it was all he would talk about whenever we had a meeting.

What she asked next, I found unbelievable. She asked why I was going after my ex-husband's pension fund. How would she know this personal financial detail? Lilith Bean went on for ten minutes about my litigation on a pension fund that really had no relevance to this conversation that should be pertaining to my daughter.

Finally, my parents returned back to our home with the kids. Lilith Bean did not even bother to interview or get further insights from them.

As she walked away, my mother said, "We're nice here; we don't abuse anybody!" Lilith did not even acknowledge her comment.

 EMOTIONAL ABUSE: *Emotional and psychological abuse in children is defined as behaviors, speech, and actions of parents, caregivers, or other significant figures in a child's life that have a negative mental impact on the child . . . Allowing children to witness the physical or emotional abuse of another.*
—Healthline, Timothy J. Legg, PhD, CRNP May

A day later, Lilith Bean went to visit my oldest son at school. My son told me about it and said that he told Lilith, "I don't have any problems with my mother; I never have!" He was anxious, tearful, and annoyed that he had been pulled out of class, and no teachers or witnesses were present when she spoke with him.

I was infuriated that Lilith would put my already anxious son through such terrible treatment, but there was nothing I could do to stop it. CPS has so much power that they can walk into a school, pull a child out of their studies, take them into a room and privately ask any questions they want. What did Lilith Bean really ask my son? Were they leading questions, like the ones she asked me? I will never know for sure, as there is no accountability in place — no checks and balances — so Lilith can say whatever she wants about what happened and she had the power to do it.

Two days later, Lilith returned again and put me and my husband through another grueling three and a half hours. Her visit was laden with more of the same accusations of my "fixation" on child abuse, and her relentless, aggressive behavior was starting to get on my nerves.

Even at work, I wasn't safe from Lilith's tirades. One day, while I was sitting at my computer during a busy day at work, I received a call. It was Lilith Bean. She yelled on the phone and threatened to take away my job, saying, "You will know the results of this indication within 40 to 60 days, and you'll hear it from me first!" I was really shaken up by this, and I'm not even sure how I gathered the courage to get off the phone. How unnecessary and unprofessional of her to call me at work! I was taking care of sick and critical patients, and this experience rattled me to the core. I worked harder than ever to focus on my patients for the rest of the day, trying to take care of them properly.

Lilith Bean's Manipulation Tactics – And Joy Fights Back

By mid-December, Lilith Bean wanted to meet me at the office of my psychologist, Jen Larson. It was a cold day, approximately one week before Christmas. My husband and Joy came with me. This time, we were coming prepared.

Lilith sat in a chair next to the door in my psychologist's conference room, and Jen Larson sat across from her. As soon as I sat down, I turned on my cell phone and held it in front of me to tape our conversation, something I wish I would've thought of doing much earlier.

Joy was extremely upset with Lilith, and she let her know exactly how she was feeling. "Why haven't you interviewed any of the family members?" she shouted. "That's part of your job, and you haven't done it. All you've done is attack Maryann and her reputation. I called you and left a message on your answering machine to call me back and you never did. Isn't that your job!" But Ms. Bean came up with one excuse after another.

When that wasn't getting anywhere, I said, "I have a witness in two of these interviews that you labeled me unstable, something you had no right to do, and talked continually about child support and a pension fund that somehow interests you, instead of my daughter, the whole time you were there."

Before I could even finish my point, Lilith Bean stood up and said, "You are indicated for emotional abuse on your daughter!"

"On what grounds?" I asked, "You don't have any real evidence for this. My daughter can live wherever she wants, anyway. She's old enough to make her own decision without getting CPS involved in it."

Lilith Bean stood up and looked at my counselor, saying under her breath. "That woman lives better than I do." She threw open the office door and fled down the long hallway.

"Have a Merry Christmas!" I shouted as she walked away.

Meanwhile, I received a letter from CPS written after the New Year. It was a letter from Lilith Bean, stating, "the evaluation was complete and it was determined that it is not necessary for your family to receive ongoing services from this agency at this time. This agency's involvement with your family will now cease."

Oddly enough, Lilith had written this letter on a Sunday. Since she was now in a supervisory position, I found it coincidental that she had written the letter on my birth date. How strange to go to work in a supervisory position on a Sunday. Everything about Lilith's involvement in this case wasn't adding up.

CPS Lies

Maryann Petri

The caseworker with the Dr. Seuss hair
Came to your house without a care,
With frivolous accusations and lies
Ready to destroy your children's lives

Anonymous phone call who could it be
An axe to grind as you can see,
Waiting for the right time to step in
She doesn't care that lying is a sin

Family Court ready there she sits
Proudly by the judge smiling like shit,
Eaten' grin she lies to and fro
Ruining your family just like so

With deceit and slander she runs her mouth
As you watch your case heading south,
"Perpetrator" on the stand as she repeats
The judge already assumes you're a deadbeat

Your reputation destroyed you have lost your job
The caseworker tells your kids you're a slob,
The other parent has much to gain
Not paying child support, now you're in pain

The lies continue she cannot stop
Perpetual lying has been her backdrop,
Now she will move on to someone new
To destroy their family for something to do

Put On Suspension For Emotional Abuse Charges

In late December, I notified my head nurse of the emotional abuse charges. Neither of us knew what to make of it at first, but when the charges for emotional abuse weren't going away, we knew we had to do something about it. She suggested I speak to the Head of Human Resources at the hospital in January. When I did so, he gave me a form that stated how indications had to be reported or the employee would be terminated. Nobody in the hospital thought I had done anything wrong, but this was the policy for anyone accused of emotional abuse. There were no exceptions.

My nursing career and everything I had worked for in the past twenty-three years was gone. The stress of knowing I may never return to my career was almost unbearable. Luckily, I stayed close to my dear friend Linda McIntire even after we stopped working together.

I applied for unemployment and received only two checks before I was denied. My daughter, my career, my income, and my self-worth were all gone. I never felt so much distress and anxiety in my life.

The hospital offered me a position on another floor, but I didn't feel like I could safely take that job because of how distressed I was. They tried to offer me jobs in other areas in the hospital that would not involve children, but, in reality, this was impossible to actually happen. Why would they want someone with an emotional abuse indication working with sick and vulnerable patients? In fact, they had ignored the Child Protective Services Law and should have never offered me any type of job.

The Child Protective Services Law, derived from the Penn State University scandal from June of 2012, made it so a person who is indicated by CPS cannot hold any job involving children. While this law was well-intentioned, it caused all sorts of problems for me and anyone who has been falsely accused of any type of child abuse.

Any job, even a home-health nursing job, could involve coming in contact with children. Imagine taking care of an elderly person when suddenly another family member drops by with grandchildren. There was simply no way I could work as a nurse until I was fully exonerated of these false allegations.

My attorney filed an appeal of the indication. We wouldn't be able to have another CPS trial until late spring, and for that entire time I could do nothing but sit at home and wait for answers, playing out a million what-if scenarios in my head. It was a miserable thing to deal with.

By March, Judge Glass was the first to look into our case, but because of a vague connection that he had with me and my husband, his intention was to back off. We were nothing more than distant acquaintances, but he clearly wanted nothing to do with our case. I was so disappointed that Judge Glass had refused to stop this ridiculous charade. To me, it felt like he was as Pontius Pilate wiping his hands clean of me and refusing to step up and end the injustice before it could go any further.

What I wish he would've said, was, "Since CPS did not remove the three younger siblings at that time, then they must not have been in any immediate danger." He could have dismissed that case without recusing himself and put the burden on CPS. Instead, Judge Glass, in his infinite wisdom—or cowardice —passed our case over into Family Court to another Judge, the Honorable Judge Mullin S. Greene. If only I had known how inaccurate the word "Honorable" was in describing that despicable man. Soon, he would tear my family apart with nothing but the stroke of a pen.

📖 TAKEAWAY:

When CPS enters your home, you are told to be cordial and accommodating. I wouldn't recommend that. I would simply tell them to contact your attorney. Discuss with your attorney if this should go right into Federal Court due to false indications instead of wallowing in the lower courts and having the case be blown out of proportion with your children being taken away from you.

CPS should never have gotten involved with my family in the way they did. A friend who worked in CPS told me that, as a general policy, they avoid getting involved in custody cases, knowing that attorneys are already involved. Funny how Lilith seemed eager to stick her nose into the situation in any way that she could, even though we already had previous issues years prior with the court with attorneys involved.

I've thought back many times on Lilith's involvement and wondered what I would do differently if this happened again. Perhaps I should have said, "I thought you were here to talk about my daughter. Instead, you only asked briefly about her whereabouts, proceeded to disclose personal information regarding a pension fund that you should know nothing about and then continuously hammered on child support litigation that had nothing to do with these allegations! How did you learn this information, and what on earth does this have to do with my daughter?" I should have asked for her supervisor's name and number and reported her.

When I spoke to Dr. Bond, one of my psychiatrists, he explained to me what he had seen happen in his practice when CPS officers got involved. "Patient-wise," he said, "they found CPS to be intrusive and ever-present, with their staff being not only incompetent and poorly trained, but doing things they should not be doing." Dr. Bond also said that "the concept of this organization was to benefit children. However, even with all their efforts, this has not been actualized in CPS. CPS does not do itself justice because what was once a nice idea...has not turned out as such."

He also felt that CPS caseworkers were milking their power to keep themselves fully funded and maintain their existence. "A lot of people found themselves intruded upon and at least 75% regret they ever had [CPS] involved in their lives." In the minority of cases in which CPS did provide a beneficial service, patients were truly grateful, but it didn't happen enough to justify all of the horrible things that have happened.

Jen Larson L.C.S.W., my counselor, said that in her patient caseload, she found CPS to be incompetent, overzealous, lazy, and biased. "They just don't bother to get all the information on cases that they are handling." Jen Larson spoke of her patients as, "Super depressed because there was no fairness, logic or right or wrong. The patients also felt helpless and hopeless and couldn't wrap their minds around what has happened in their lives."

Jen Larson also observed that the courts were "dropping the ball" and there were no repercussions for their actions. She states, "It's frustrating for my clients, and they complain that their attorneys would then send in an underling or a beginner to handle the case, sometimes without any warning, when the attorney they trusted didn't want to argue in front of a certain judge." I told her this had happened in my case as well.

Jen told me some clients were treated so unfairly in the courtroom that one parent only gets to see their child for 24 hours every two weeks, while another client, a father, was not getting custody when the mother was abusing drugs at random while taking the children and never informing the father, making the excuse that she "couldn't find him."

Family Court At Its Finest

"Parental Alienation is...a profound form of psychological trauma experienced by targeted parents...The fact that children witness such abuse of a parent also makes alienation a form of child abuse."

-Edward Kruk Ph.D.

"All we want is to be able to see our boys," my elderly father stood in the hallway and said to my daughter as she stood by Seth, right before the trial began.

"You will," she assured my father. Soon, however, I would learn that my daughter had no intention of keeping that promise.

I entered the courtroom and sat down. My ex-husband and his wife, along with their extended family, sat to the left of me. Two psychologists and Lilith Bean sat with them, shoulder-to-shoulder, laughing and talking as if they were a part of the family. The behavior was completely unprofessional.

Judge Greene came to the bench, went over the pension fund issue, quickly dismissed it, and began discussing the Emergency Petition for Special Relief. Then, Attorney Black called Lilith Bean to the witness stand. Lilith walked to her place with a spring in her step and a slight smile, clearly enjoying the attention.

When Attorney Black asked Lilith Bean what her capacity had been at CPS, Ms. Bean replied, "Currently, I'm a supervisor. However, when I assessed this case, I was an intake clinician."

Attorney Black asked her, "In your twelve years serving as an intake clinician, how many times have you indicated a report of emotional abuse?"

Lilith Bean replied, "Me, personally, one—this case."

Lilith said my daughter told her she was experiencing anxiety, depression, and suicidal ideations. My daughter blamed all of these feelings on me speaking negatively about her father. According to Lilith, I would reprimand my daughter verbally, ground her, or remove items whenever she tried to defend him.

I couldn't believe what I was hearing. Everything that Lilith had said was completely made up! I had never even spoke about their father in our home, let alone punished her for defending him! Already, I could see where this case was headed — and it wasn't in the direction of truth or justice.

Miss Bean insisted that my daughter was "very emotionally upset," "mature," (That wouldn't be the last time I would hear her described that way), and wished I would get help for my problems.

Then, Lilith went on to describe her visit with me, which she called "bizarre in nature." Lilith said I was "completely fixated" on my husband and his wife, saying that I "could not get [myself] to pull...out of that mode of thinking and...focus on what we needed to do for the children." She painted me out to be some sort of crazy person, unable to refrain from talking negatively about Seth, even in front of the kids. She said my sons had told her they thought I needed help as well, and my oldest son had been particularly humiliated when they had to be driven around in a car with a sign stating that their father was a "deadbeat dad." It didn't seem to matter that I had already addressed what this sign really said to

Lilith. That didn't fit her narrative, so she created her own version of what happened.

Later, Attorney Black asked Lilith the most devastating question any parent could hear, "Based upon your twelve years of working through CPS and your interaction with the children in this case as well as the mom, do you believe it is in the children's best interest to be with mom at this point?"

"I do not," Lilith said, smiling slightly.

When explaining why, Ms. Bean said that when someone is indicated for emotional abuse, CPS looks at the parents to see if "they first acknowledge the abuse," and that I couldn't acknowledge it. Lilith also said that she tried to offer tools to help me get out of the rut I was in, but I refused to even have a conversation with her about it. "And I spent hours talking to her... hours!" she said. Ms. Bean also reported that my sons said they were punished by me if they defended their dad as well.

Attorney Black asked, "Was there an incident that occurred relative to her singing at the library that you were made aware of?"

Ms. Bean answered, "Yes." She then said that my daughter had been afraid to even mention singing at the library in the first place "because it was near the courthouse." Well, that was a first. According to Ms. Bean, I told my daughter that if she sang at the library, then she didn't love me. She mentioned some text messages that we had sent back and forth and said that the entire exchange was "bizarre."

"Did Ms. Petri ever indicate to you whether she would stop coming after Mr. Seth Balor?" Attorney Black asked.

"She said she would never quit, and it was game on."

Lilith Bean was cross-examined by my attorney, who tried to expose the truth of what had happened. My attorney questioned why no crisis plan had been put in place if my daughter had suicidal ideations, and why this had not been addressed in a professional setting.

Ms. Bean skated the question and essentially said that the suicidal ideations weren't current so she hadn't done anything about it.

I was shocked. If my child was experiencing suicidal ideations, then why wasn't this addressed in a professional setting? How was it that one day my daughter was having suicidal ideations, and then the next day she was fine? Rule of thumb is that people actually commit suicide when they appear to be feeling better.

Not only did my daughter share text messages between me and her with Ms. Bean, she also shared ones between my ex-husband and myself. My attorney wanted to know why Mr. Balor would have forwarded these conversations to a child.

Ms. Bean stated, "because there was so much fear of letting her know that this was occurring."

"That he decided to involve her in the middle of it?" my attorney interrupted.

"That would be a question for him," Lilith said bitterly.

After a few more questions, my attorney stepped down and Attorney Black took back the stage. He asked Ms. Bean if she thought I had serious boundary issues with my kids, and she said "yes." She also insisted that Seth's home was a completely safe environment for the kids to live in.

Then, Judge Greene asked Ms. Bean a variety of questions, including whether or not the kids were safe physically in my home (they were), if the grandparents were a positive influence in their lives (according to her, this was the only time that I didn't speak negatively about their dad), and if the father ever talked negatively about me (according to her, the kids said that this never happened).

That concluded the examination process of Lilith Bean. I wondered where all of these lies had come from. Hearing her use the word, "fixation," over and over and over again had been maddening. There was a fixation, alright, and Lilith had focused it straight on me.

"Before we close the testimony, I want my client to testify," my attorney said. He spoke about the alleged emotional abuse and said that I had filed an appeal to that finding.

My attorney then helped me confront Ms. Bean's allegations and share what had actually happened. I also described Ms. Bean's verbal abuse and how she had threatened to take away my job.

After my attorney finished questioning me, it was Attorney Black's turn. "Let me get this straight, Ms. Petri. Your testimony is that Lilith Bean's testimony was a fabrication?" I agreed. Attorney Black went on, throwing his hands into the air as he asked, "What plausible reason would she have to come in and perjure herself? Is it out of some allegiance to Judith Baylor; do you believe that?"

"Yeah, I don't know," I said. "I hope not."

Attorney Black continued, saying, "Your daughter thinks you need help; your oldest son thinks you need help; Ms. Bean thinks you need help; you're the only person involved in this case who doesn't see that you have a problem and that you are the problem. Do you see that?"

"I wish I would have brought my kids." I said. But as I look back on that hearing, I don't think it would have made a difference. The outcome had been planned out before I had even entered the courtroom.

Attorney Black continued, asking leading questions, accusing me of things I had never done, and interrupting me whenever he didn't like where I was going, all with no objections from the judge. He stated that my son had started counseling because of my behavior, even though this wasn't the case — he had gone for anger management. He stated that we had begun co-parenting counseling because the kids were having problems with my parenting, not Seth's, even though it was both of our parenting and Seth was the one that had eventually refused to go. I was perfectly willing to restart co-parenting counseling at any time.

At one point, when I told Attorney Black that I believed Seth was planting accusations about me "needing help" in the kid's heads, he pranced in front of the area before the witness stand and said, "Not a single expert witness would testify to that, would you agree? I tell you what, I have a proposal for you; why don't you agree to the temporary order putting your kids in with Mr. Balor and go through a custody evaluation?"

"No!" I said, "my kids wouldn't be able to handle being away from me."

Once Attorney Black was finished, Judge Greene started asking questions regarding my career, level of education, and what department I worked on. Then, the Judge quietly asked me, "Are you...taking any kind of medication?"

"Just Ativan for my nerves." I told him, and that I also used it to help me sleep after coming home from long shifts.

Judge Greene asked what was wrong with my nerves, and I told him that I had a lot to be upset about with everything going on, and I was just trying to find a way to cope.

As the questioning continued, and I realized that Judge Greene had little interest in knowing the truth, I said, "I want you to know that my kids love me very much, and they would not want to be separated from me."

These questions were getting monotonous now and the lies were absolutely sickening. When Attorney Black interviewed Ms. Bean again, she insisted over and over again that my kids were not safe living with me.

When my attorney asked Ms. Bean what action was taken, and if she had offered any further services in Ms. Petri's home, Ms. Bean stated, "What played out was Jen Larson and I had a conversation. I expressed my concern about her engaging in any kind of family therapy until she first resolves her own issues. It is clear to me that Ms. Petri's obsession, fixation, I don't know, whatever you want to call it clinically, would directly interfere with her ability to, or her kids to want to sit down with her and address those issues until she resolved whatever was going on with herself."

My attorney questioned Ms. Bean further, and eventually asked if that was her recommendation or Jen Larson's recommendation. Ms. Bean stated, "Both."

What Ms. Bean had just said was the real work of fiction. Later, Jen told me that she had never said that! Any good counselor would recommend family counseling, especially at a time like this.

Attorney Black asked Ms. Bean, "Until the emotional issues that Ms. Petri has are resolved, is it a safe environment for the kids?"

"I don't think so," Ms. Bean said, again with that smug smile drawn across her face.

At that time, the Judge wanted to speak to my daughter with both attorneys present, so they left to go to the room where my daughter waited for them.

When I passed Lilith Bean in the pews, I was so angry that I called her a liar to her face. She postured and said, "What did you say Maryann?"

"I don't remember." I said.

Daughter's Testimony

I didn't expect the questioning with my daughter to go well. Clearly, she was coached and had an ax to grind. She told the judge that I blamed her father for not having any money, and that this was why I was so angry. My daughter said, "she doesn't care about me or my brothers. She might think she does, she might act like it, but she doesn't and that's a shame. But she—it's like so much— toxic environment. I don't know how else to describe it."

My daughter also recommended, "if my brothers came to live with my dad, I think they would be upset at first, but...they would all just benefit from it. And I hate to say it, but she needs to get some help before she can have children in her care like that. I don't know that any help would help her, but I don't think she should be around them right now. My therapist told me to spend more time with her. So I would come downstairs sometimes and watch TV with her and something, and nothing happened. It just made it worse, if anything."

After interviewing my daughter, Judge Greene came back to the bench and said, "Here we heard from the daughter who is sixteen, obviously very bright, very intelligent, very mature, very candid, very well-reasoned in her judgment. And she clearly wants to stay with her father..." then, he continued, "I don't get the feeling that she is anything other than a typical teenager who is going through some significant trauma in the home. So I'm going to defer to her, obviously, and I'll respect her wishes and give what she said about her siblings not ultimate weight, but some significant weight as well."

Judge Greene continued, "I make the finding that the mother is trying to turn the children against the father, for whatever reason, and that...it's severe."

Judge Greene then said that my ex-husband was "more likely to maintain a loving, stable, consistent and nurturing relationship with the children adequate for their emotional needs," that I was unstable, and that my "fabricated" testimony about Lilith Bean was proof that I was in denial.

"So for those reasons," Judge Greene said, "I'm going to enter an order...that all three children be placed with their father."

Everyone on my ex-husband's side of the family, including Lilith Bean, clapped, laughed, whooped, and cheered. The judge did nothing to stop them. He never slammed down his gavel. Was this all some sort of game to them? Had they taken me away from my children, manipulated the court hearings, and painted me out to be some sort of monster just because? I thought about my boys, who were expecting me to pick them up from school, and how devastated they would be when they heard the news. How could they do something so hurtful to the boys and cheer about it?

Judge Greene put me under a no-contact order, saying that I would have no contact with my children via landline, cell phone, or iPad; not even on holidays. The order was temporary until I could get my "mental health" in order, but I would be allowed some visitations with my kids.

Attorney Black recommended that I get a psychiatric evaluation, and Judge Greene agreed. Then, he said, "I don't want to keep you from your kids, but I have to look out for what I think is best for them, based on what I'm hearing today... I'm going to give you every opportunity to address this. So let's start by continuing to see Jen Larson, get an updated psychiatric evaluation." He did not, however, recommend that my ex-husband get an evaluation as well at that time.

My life was hanging in the balance of an exonerated outcome on the CPS hearing. As my attorney and I left the courtroom, I saw Judith, tissue in hand, speaking with her sisters with tears in her eyes weeping. One minute she was cheering at the news, and now she's crying? Now there's someone that needed a psychiatric evaluation.

I closed the bedroom doors to my boys' rooms as soon as I came home. The very thought of looking inside there, of seeing all the happy times that once were, was more than I could handle. Nightmares about that hearing would haunt me for years to come. I even recall awaking to my own voice stating, "I object Judge Greene."

 TAKEAWAY:

Award-winning investigative journalist Keith Harmon Snow states, "Rich, poor, middle-class—no child in America is safe." On their watch, each year, hundreds of thousands of children suffer from abuse (including rape and prolonged torture) that would not happen without the corrupt practices taking place in CPS and Family Court.

As you will soon discover court officials heavily profit from these induced conflicts. They have learned how to milk the system for financial gain, by targeting the protective "fit" parent instead of the abusive "unfit" parent. This is because the fit parent will go to court case after court case to get their children back and will spend a lot more money than an unfit parent ever would on caring for them. Although the State will pay court officials for low-income families, the system forces fit parents who are middle class or wealthier to foot the bills for all court services. Thus, they are making big business from using desperate and vulnerable parents and the children as currency.

All across the country, good children are being placed with pedophiles, sadistic sociopaths, and narcissists. This is what happened to me; but, most importantly, this is what happened to my children. They were ripped away from the mother who loved them, having all contact with me taken away from them, and forced to live with a narcissistic father and step mother who cared more about manipulating their own children into hating their mother than they did about their children's wellbeing.

The false allegations and indications brought on by CPS affected my children deeply. They were severely embarrassed and even taunted about what was being said and rumored about myself while at school by their classmates. The changes worsened with their cheerfulness dying, their once happy, carefree faces were now permanently saddened with a flat affect when the lies came out about myself and that destroyed their inner peace. At school and even in the other home they were conflicted and felt they had to defend me, the parent that was being "picked on." CPS caused mass havoc in their lives and extremely high anxiety levels that they should not have had to deal with at their stages in their lives. They should have been left to enjoy their childhoods and their friends, not worrying about court issues and transcripts being read to them by their father with a psychologist present.

When our Happiness Ended

Maryann Petri

How many people have happy lives
I sit around and wonder,
Watching people with their families
Thinking back when my children were younger

What happy times we had at the pool
Memories of parks and swings,
By the lake picking out beach glass
Not knowing CPS was waiting in the wings

Getting ready for school in the morning
In our cozy beach house that was blue,
With two cats chasing and catching mice
Years later not knowing what CPS was up to

That year ended all our happiness
And the dreams of my dear children,
Falsehoods entwined with so many lies
CPS perjured itself in Family Court then

Many four-faced family members
And those also working in the courthouse,
Always creating havoc in the courtroom
While the corrupt judge ruled like a powerhouse

Cheering and clapping when his order came down
The judge did not slam down his gavel,
Friends with attorneys as it turned out
The judge listened intently to CPS lies unravel

Years have passed and their emotions destroyed
Shattered from lies and heartache,
Couldn't they think of the children first
Instead of themselves just for their sake?

The Disaster of the Ruling

Maryann Petri

There was a time but I don't know when
The children were happy and were with their families then,
Until CPS wallowed in filth yet arose to great power
Taking children away from a parent and making them cower

False allegations here and character defamation there
A Target-parent in continuous litigation out of fear,
Fraudulent accusations force you to clear your name
The cost of lies and litigation is the goal of the game

Who can dream up what next while they lay awake at night
Scheming to make your life a living Hell and a court fight,
Better defend yourself, protect and shield your little one
As CPS or the Narcissist will put you through another rerun

Of Courtroom Hell to clear your name in hopes to see your kids
An obstacle course or a gauntlet and yet the judge forbids,
Any time, holiday or weekend, no contact he will rule
Looking at the judge on the bench, what a piece of stool

What will it be you wonder and ponder in time
Possibly serving time for something that wasn't a crime,
No expectations as you watch your children being placed
When none of this should have happened, such a big disgrace

PART THREE:
Taking The Kids Wasn't Enough

My New Normal

"If a child is being physically or sexually abused, would people turn a blind eye and ignore it? Well Parental Alienation is just as damaging as physical or sexual abuse. Just because you can't see the bruises or the scars, they are there on the inside. Don't look the other way, speak out. Many of the general public do not know about Parental Alienation and that needs to change."

– Stephen Best

I had lost everything. I was unemployed, childless, waiting for the next trial and holding onto hope that I could get my children back, if only for a small amount of time. I had a lot of time on my hands and nothing to do with it except wait.

Shortly after the no-contact order was given, my oldest son tried to call me on his father's landline, and I quickly answered my cell. All I heard was "Mom!" and loud voices in the background. Someone took the phone away from him and slammed it down.

Around the same time, my oldest son demanded to see me on his birthday. So his father allowed my husband and me to visit and give him his present. I brought the twins a small gift as well. When we came over, Brad stood in the kitchen doorway. My son ran over to give me a hug, crying. Seth was never more than five feet away, always watching. When I hugged my kids, I whispered to them, "Speak the truth." My oldest son opened his present of Swedish Fish, Peach Rings and several other of his favorite candy, along with a birthday card with money in it. We only stayed ten minutes because Seth stood there, just five feet away, monitoring our every move.

My parents wanted to see the children, but they couldn't deal with Seth listening in on their every word. They were 76 and 74 at the time. It was pathetic that they had to deal with such degrading treatment at their age.

My son also attempted to contact me via iPad. I knew that I wasn't supposed to speak with him, but my heart was broken, and I couldn't bring myself to ignore a message from my own son. We exchanged a few words via Instagram before that source of communication was cut off as well. He also tried to contact me via Snapchat, but I didn't really understand how to use it.

Judge Greene authorized visits in April between the kids and relatives on my side of the family, but Seth's family members refused to transport my children to me. My attorney filed another petition that gave me designated days and hours with my kids. Seth did not follow these rules either. When I took my father with me to pick up the children, no one was home. We called the State Police and filed a report, but all they would do is call the "D.A. on call" who would recommend another Family Court hearing. Unable to do anything else, my father and I drove home, where my mother had already set the table for us and the boys. Sitting at that table was positively heartbreaking. Seth was now in contempt of court, but Judge Greene did nothing about it.

I was terrified when I was labeled as an abuser that my friends and family would treat me differently, but, luckily, they were incredibly compassionate. They saw through the façade and gave me the support I needed. To this day, however, I can't understand what I did to my daughter that caused her to go to such lengths to hurt me.

I wonder what would've changed if I had recognized the signs of Parental Alienation earlier. Looking back, it's clear that this process was years in the making. Several months earlier, my daughter came down from her room and told me she wanted to go on birth control. I told her she would have to see a gynecologist, because our family had a history of endometriosis. She was furious, shouting, "I want to go live with dad!" I told her to go to her room and cool off, but she was relentless. "Then I'm going to call the judge!" she shouted.

Shocked by my daughter's comment, I called my ex-husband to discuss it with him. He informed me that he had taken her to the family physician that afternoon and discussed the birth control pill, but decided that I should handle it since I was a nurse. My ex-husband and daughter had intentionally put me in a no-win situation.

I barely saw my daughter that evening, but I did go upstairs to hug her goodnight at bedtime. She hugged me back but hardly spoke, and remained distant and quiet for the next couple of weeks. When my parents came over with their dinners on Thursday, she would not eat with us. She was intentionally secluding herself, a classic sign of Parental Alienation in progress. After my daughter left for the last time, I texted her and told her that I loved her and would always be there for her. She has never responded or contacted me since.

When my sons were taken away, a friend told me my daughter was going around her high school telling friends and teachers that I needed help and was mentally ill. I was horrified. Another friend told me that the parents at the school were very aware of my daughter's "cleverness." I knew what they meant. When my daughter lived with me, she would date one boyfriend after another for as little as two weeks at a time, cycling through them as soon as she had what she wanted or became bored.

Several weeks after my daughter left, my oldest son told me he needed to get some colored pencils from his sister's room. It took him a while to return, but when he did, his bag was full of items from my daughter's room. Clearly, either my daughter or Seth had asked my son to gather these things for him and to lie about what he was really doing. I was horrified. I texted Seth, telling him that all he had to do was tell me what my daughter needed, and I would get it for them — he didn't have to get my son to lie about it! His response? "Okay."

About a week before Christmas, Brad's family got together. It would be a sad reunion as my beloved mother-in-law had passed away from cancer a few weeks earlier. Joy came over to help me clean and straighten up my daughter's room, and we put the rest of her clothing that she hadn't cared to take with her into a black garbage bag. As we cleaned, Joy and I found empty beer bottles and wine cooler bottles shoved into the sleeves of an old zip-up sweatshirt. I took pictures of them and notified her psychologist. She said that she would talk to my daughter about this in their next meeting. In that meeting, the psychologist encouraged my daughter to talk to me and include me in the sessions; that it would be a huge mistake to throw me away. My daughter wanted nothing to do with me.

📖 TAKEAWAY:

My child, once happy, suddenly became moody and resentful. When Brad and I purchased our home, my oldest son, in his late teens, came in for a tour. He had a flat, sad expression and did not show any emotion regarding moving into a new home with his own room. In fact, he resented it. Brad and I found a refrigerator that was more than half off the sale price and had a touch screen feature. This appalled my oldest son, saying to me over the phone, "Do you really need a touch screen refrigerator? Really?" The conversation spiraled downward with expletives, and he told me that he wished I would die for my birthday. He knew what kind of mother I was and all the happy years I gave him. I tried bringing up memories only three to six years prior and he had no recollection. He told me that Judith was his real mother, not me.

Several years prior, when I was allowed to see my children every other weekend, my kids were in their mid-teens. They wanted to sleep over from Sunday night to Monday. When I was supposed to drop them off at their father's house, my sons called their father to let him know they wanted to sleep over and would see him after school. He was infuriated, sending my sons rapid texts and angry phone calls.

My youngest son called his father an expletive, turned off his phone and came out in the living room to watch TV. My oldest son, however, was more pliable. Seth continuously called him. At one point my son came towards me, and I heard Seth yell over the cell phone, "If you don't come home tonight, I'm going to put your mother in jail and you'll never see her again!!" My son and I just looked at each other. My son then revealed to me that their father talked badly about me constantly when they were with him. My son looked at me, tears streaming down his face. "It's always like this at home," he said, "They're always talking about how horrible you are." I was sick to my stomach. I wondered how long it would take for them to dislike me, too.

I told my sons that this wasn't going to work. Had my oldest son just turned his phone off like his younger siblings did, maybe it would have turned out differently. I told my children I would walk them out to his car. My oldest son wept and said, "I'm sorry."

In an article written by Julio Rivera on August 12, 2019, titled, "Do Family Courts Encourage Child Abuse?" Rivera writes, "Are Family Courts places where justice and fairness are meted out, or are they enablers of bias, abuse or even fraud? Everyone agrees, and statistics bear out, that children who have both parents involved in their upbringing tend to fare better than those who do not."

Rivera continues, "The very nature of the adversarial court system may be encouraging an insidious form of child abuse called Parental Alienation. Parental Alienation involves the idea that one parent, through his or her conduct or negative feelings towards the other parent, has influenced their child to the point that the child actually rejects the other parent. Family Court may exacerbate Parental Alienation, as parents seek advantage in custody and financial support during divorce proceedings."

California Judge Donald B. King stated, "The role of the Family Law Court too often is to shoot the survivors."

Dr. Sol Goldstein, a Child Psychiatrist with four decades of experience in treating Parental Alienation, calls it "the worst form of child abuse." Goldstein adds, "It's causing distortions in the mind and the distortions also work on the character, it alters the character of the child, so later on they have difficulties of every level of interpersonal relationships and personal thoughts about themselves. It's the most awful form of abuse and has to be recognized as such."

"Alienated parents are more than twice as likely to die from suicide than a parent who has their children in their lives. In the U.K. more than 100 people take their own lives every week, and it is a certainty that being alienated from their children is a significant factor in many of these suicides."

- STEPHEN BEST

Emotional Disaster

Maryann Petri

The outcome of disaster
Has been written on the plaster,
Happiness is shattered
But what was it that mattered

Children's faces forever searching
Hands clasped for a family yearning,
Family Court destroyers abundant
Orders no contact so very redundant

What mattered were their lives
Wanting parents but not severed ties,
Allowed to love both mom and dad
Intentionally kept away from either is sad

So the outcome is truly a disaster
 From children growing up so much faster,
Playing adult games with consequences
Using drugs and alcohol and not defenseless

Uncaring and disconnected they will be
Emotionally vacant and not at all carefree,
Wanting to live their lives together as a happy family
Forever searching and now an emotional casualty

Exonerated:
Well, At Least For Four Days

 Legal Abuse: *an unfair legal action that has been
initiated with malicious and selfish intentions. Abuse
can originate from nearly any part of the legal system,
including frivolous and vexatious litigants, abuses
by law enforcement, incompetent, careless or corrupt
attorneys and misconduct for the judiciary itself.*

That Spring, the CPS hearing finally arrived. It lasted the entire
day. Lilith Bean was interviewed on the witness stand, using the
word "fixation" and "perpetrator" countless times. I was treated
like a criminal and labeled guilty until proven innocent.

When the judge interviewed Seth, he wept on the stand,
saying, "I just wanted to keep the kids safe." To my relief, this
judge was not as quick to believe him as Judge Greene. He
questioned my daughter, saying something to the effect of, "I'm
missing pieces of the puzzle here. It sounds to me like support to
contradiction or—yeah, forget it , it ain't happening. There's just
something missing there."

When I was on the stand, I explained once again how Lilith
Bean had treated me to the point of verbal abuse. He asked me in

a compassionate and concerned voice, "Why didn't you ask her to leave?" If only I had known that I could safely do that at the time!

I stated, "You know what? I never had CPS at my door. I was afraid to upset her because she had so much power that I didn't know if I asked her to leave, she might really do something to me, like take my boys away." Had I only known and that is exactly what happened.

There were a few exchanges of words between the attorneys, and then the hearing was over. Now, all I could do was wait for the outcome and hope for the best. I was exonerated of the emotional abuse indication. What a relief; I could finally get back to work and do the things that I loved! On that very day, I let the hospital and my friend Linda know. She was ecstatic and took me out to lunch to celebrate. Unfortunately, our celebration wouldn't last for long.

It's Happening Again

Only four days later, I received another call from CPS. A caseworker, Mara Smith, spoke to me with a rude and abrasive tone. I stopped her in the middle of her tirade and told her that I wouldn't tolerate her behavior. If she was going to talk to me like that, she could speak to my attorney. I hung up, my heart racing. I had to call the hospital, my friends, my family, and let them know that this wasn't over after all.

One week later, Mara Smith called back, this time with a kinder demeanor. She made small talk, and then, out of nowhere, casually let me know that I was being indicated on an emotional abuse charge on my oldest son. "What on earth for?" I asked, shocked at what I was hearing. Mara told me it was because I wouldn't let my son ride his bike around the block, and I had taken away his X-Box.

I couldn't believe it. My sons were not even in my care when this new indication of emotional abuse was made. Yes, we had supervised visits, but those ended at the beginning of Summer. When would I have had the opportunity to take his X-box or even see him ride his bike in our neighborhood? Even if I had, how did this constitute emotional abuse? We got off the phone, and I called my attorney, who filed an appeal. The bills from all of these hearings were mounting higher and higher.

When paperwork for the indication came in the mail, I read that my oldest son had told the caseworker, "I don't see the point in this." Also he refused to continue to speak to her. I couldn't believe that they were dragging my son through this nonsense. My friends and family were appalled when they heard the news.

I received a letter from Mara Smith that was dated mid Spring-time, even though she had sent it months later. It said, "this agency received a referral regarding your children and I was assigned to evaluate the allegations. I have completed my evaluation and have determined that it is not necessary for your family to receive ongoing services from this agency at this time. This agency's involvement with your family will now cease."

Unexpected Child Support Claims

Then, a letter from Domestic Relations came, saying I owed $2,800.00 in arrears. I had never heard anything about these arrears until then! I called the Domestic Relations department and a woman told me, "Yes, I remember, as soon as your ex-husband got the judge's custody order in the mail, on the same day, he came down here and filed for child support on you." I was horrified. Seth expected approximately $1000.00 a month in child support, including arrears knowing I had been suspended from my nursing job?

All I could do was wait and appeal. Distraught and powerless to change anything, I slept on the couch during the day, and my depression and anxiety reached an all-time high.

In his book, *Preserving Family Ties*, Dr. Roseman writes, "When two working parents share the household, income is generally greater than if one parent works. When a parent is absent from the household, both parents suffer economically. The absent or non-custodial parent also struggles to provide child support while meeting his or her own survival needs. Clearly, economic stress is greatly heightened for both parents, though (nontaxable) child support payments offer some relief to the custodial parent.

I tried to stay busy. I painted a picture of a horse on the beach using oils. I made some fun videos on judges on my YouTube channel. I graced Facebook asking for prayers to get me out of this situation and for it all to end soon. If I wasn't sleeping I was painting, making humorous comments on social media, listening to the school gossip.

Second Emotional Abuse Court Case- Judge Green Refuses To Recuse Himself

In my last hearing with Judge Green, I learned that he had a close relationship with Attorney Black, having worked together in a department of the courthouse for years. I believed this was a major conflict of interest, and I knew that I would never have a fair trial with him in charge, so I complained to the Administrative Office of Courts, insisting he be recused. "The case couldn't be more rigged than it already was, so what harm would it do?" My attorneys asked.

This only proved to irritate Judge Green, and he insisted that he was not that close with Attorney Black. Judge Greene asked me,

"Ms. Petri, I am asking if you do want me off this case.... No, it's up to you. Don't look at your attorneys. It's up to you to ask."

"I believe you should be off this case," I said firmly. Of course, Judge Greene denied my request.

During a previous hearing in May, Judge Greene ordered both my ex-husband and myself to undergo a psychiatric evaluation. My attorneys were very happy with my results. To Judge Greene's dismay, however, Seth had not bothered to get one.

When my attorney questioned the psychologist, an independent contractor, Dr Abbott, about my evaluation, he said that I was honest, open, and very "anxious and worried about problems [I] was faced with." He said that a lot of it was reactive, but that "there was an underlying anxiety disorder." He continued to add, however, that "Anxiety is the epidemic of our age" and that it would in no way keep me from being a good parent.

Attorney Black asked the psychologist about the medication other physicians had put me on. He questioned, "her behavior has escalated; do you still believe that it is an effective method to treat her anxiety disorder?"

Dr Abbott did not fall for Attorney Black's leading question. "I didn't have evidence of her behavior escalating," he said.

Attorney Black also asked if he thought it was wise that I had posted about Parental Alienation online. The psychologist answered, "Unfortunately, in my view that's not a psychological issue. It becomes a legal issue. As far as this goes, I've seen this before. A lot of people are very concerned that their children are being affected by Parental Alienation Syndrome. It's just so common, I hesitate to make a lot more of it."

In the written report, the psychologist argued that my behavior suggested that it was my husband that needed a psychological evaluation and to be investigated.

Seth Is Questioned

The psychologist was dismissed and the court went into recess. Upon returning, the opposing counsel was trying to get in contact with my oldest son's psychologist, who was late for the hearing. So to kill time, Attorney Black called my ex-husband on the stand and questioned him about how things were going at home with the boys.

Seth said that my oldest son had been depressed and angry after being separated from me, lashing out at his brothers and sister, and that they were concerned that this behavior wasn't normal. "So that's why we started looking to other causes," he said.

The source Seth should've looked at was himself. It's common knowledge that kids who are taken away from their mother will act out. Yes, I had a small amount of contact with my son, but this was not the cause of his behavior.

Seth twisted things around, straight up lied, coached the kids to say what he wanted, and did it all before an inept judge who soaked it up like a sponge. The lies Seth regurgitated on the stand would be more than enough to infuriate Lady Justice. But where was Lady Justice now? I just wished it could all be over. My husband was just as frustrated with Family Court as I was. He once said to me, "Every time you go into court; we lose. Where is God?" I understood why he felt this way, but I never stopped praying. One of my favorite quotes that I got from Carolyn Pershing is, "My God is not in a hurry, but He is never late."

Later, my attorney showed Seth a copy of Judge Greene's order and pointed out the portion that talked about a visitation schedule. My attorney stated, "You didn't attempt to work with Ms. Petri in setting up that visitation schedule, did you?"

Seth argued that he couldn't find anyone to supervise the meetings, even though they didn't need to be supervised, and that he didn't believe the visitation schedule was reasonable. He said the reason he disobeyed the orders was because he didn't believe it was appropriate for my sons to see me since I had broken the no-contact order. Everything he had done was either at the advice of his lawyers or in the best interest of his kids........ Right.

At one point, my attorney had his hands to his side, shaking his head in disbelief, and said, "And that's what you forced us to do, was to file a motion for visitation; is that correct?"

That was exactly it! Seth wanted to force me back into court. I was financially tapped out and tired of this nonsense.

Seth stated, "I did not force it. Her actions forced it."

Seth skated around each question as if he was above the law — and maybe he actually was, given everything that he had gotten away with.

Maryann Is Questioned Again

Attorney Black was waiting for my son's psychologist, so he asked me to come to the witness stand again. He asked incredibly intrusive questions about my doctors, medications, and what I was seeing my counselor for, trying to find holes in my testimony. He, again, questioned me about my use of social media. I apologized to the court for the mistake I made in contacting my son and explained that he had reached out to me, and I couldn't ignore that, and told them that I had ceased all contact since early summer.

Attorney Black asked, "Now, would you agree that you have a defiant personality?"

"No, I do not."

Attorney Black asked, "Do you believe that you are persecuted?"

"Yes, I question that," I said.

Attorney Black went on, "Because I'd like to ask a couple of questions. I mean, every time you've had an adverse ruling against you, you make a complaint. Is that a fair statement?"

Apparently, Judge Greene had lost track of what was happening. "Wait, who?" he asked.

Attorney Black continued, ignoring the judge's question. "Okay. Let's go back. Judge Speer, in a separate proceeding issued an order you didn't like, and you filed a complaint with the disciplinary board against him; is that correct?"

I agreed.

Attorney Black asked, "Lilith Bean, who is the CPS intake officer who first reviewed your daughter's complaint, and I believe also had involvement with your son's complaint, you filed a complaint against her with the Department of Public Welfare of something like that?"

I told Attorney Black who I was referring to, "The Honorable...."

Attorney Black, with all his dramatics lifted his arms into the air, looking up at the ceiling and shouted, "And who is he?!"

The courtroom burst into laughter, so much so that I had to wait for the laughter to fade in order to answer. When I did, I leaned into the microphone and dragged out my answer, "The Governor ...of the state of ...Connecticut." Even the stenographer looked up at me nodding and broadly smiled.

He looked back at me in a state of shock, jaw dropped, and went to sit down at his desk in the court room. No gavel was slammed down. Once the laughter subsided, he got back up and asked, "And you also received information from the Connecticut Department of Human Services, correct, a letter relative to your complaint?"

I replied, "Yes."

"And you also sent a letter when this judge ruled against you to the Administrative Office of Courts complaining about his conduct; is that correct? Now that makes three individuals— actually let's go back because before I got involved in this case you filed a complaint with the disciplinary board against my wife, who was previous counsel?" Attorney Black asked.

I answered with a slight smile, "There were two complaints."

Attorney Black asked, "Two complaints. When are you going to file one against me?"

Now that's a stupid question, I thought. He walked right into that one. "Maybe, in a matter of time. I mean, I'm not sure. What I do is stand up for myself."

Attorney Black got up to stand, "Okay, but do you find it somewhat concerning at all that, number one, every complaint that you filed has been rejected and, number two, that you only do things when things don't go your way?"

I replied that the Governor's office did take command over my complaint against CPS. "What I'm saying is that I'm a nurse, and I'm a patient advocate. And I had to be an advocate for anyone, including myself."

The Oldest Son Is Questioned

Suddenly all four of my children appeared. "Come on, sit up front in the front row here." The judge said. He then explained to the kids how they would be interviewed, sequestered and that he wanted to talk to my oldest son first.

Once he was in a private room with my oldest son, Judge Greene said, "You understand that, unfortunately, your parents are still involved in a dispute over visitation with you and your brothers essentially, right?"

"Yes," my son said.

Judge Greene asked him, "You live with your dad now, and it's you, your brothers and older sister. You are also going to be a freshman in high school. How are things going with your father?"

My oldest son answered, "I think it's been...worse."

Judge Greene asked, "What do you mean by that?" Upon reading this, I would think a seasoned judge would be adept to knowing what my son was stating. What a mess, and he still didn't get it. Instead he turned the conversation onto the usage of social media. The judge used social media as a crutch. Plain and simple. He didn't care about my son's wellbeing. He was in it with the opposing attorney to fix the case to their own benefit.

My son answered, "I miss my mom..."

Judge Green then asked my son when was the last time he saw me. Then, he went on to question him about his use of social media. By the time he admitted to contacting me in secret, he had begun to cry.

Judge Greene asked, "How come? Why? It's okay. I'm not mad...I don't mean to upset you, buddy. I really don't. I'm trying to figure this out. Is it because you really want to talk to her and see her?"

My son answered, "yes."

Judge Green, getting back to the business at hand, quickly asked my son, "Do you think your mother has some problems and can you tell me what your take on that is, what you think?"

My son, obviously coached, answered "Well, I think she has like—oh, I don't think she knows what she's doing. Like some things she does, I don't think she knows what she's doing."

Judge Greene prodded, "How do you think she can take care of you then? Or is it more like you want to be there for her?"

My son answered, "I just want to be there for her."

Judge Greene later asked him, "Do you want to—who do you want to live with?"

My son answered, "My mom." Judge Greene asked him why, and he said it was because mom was nicer.

"What do you mean? She lets you do whatever you want?" Judge Greene asked, clearly trying to get evidence against me.

"No," my son replied, "...I just like the way she treats us and stuff. Nicer than...my dad. I just like hanging out with my mom more than my dad."

The judge asked my son a little bit more about his mental health and what medications he was taking. But the real zinger was when Judge Green asked, "You're okay seeing the psychologist for a while, even though your mother doesn't want you to?"

The judge had put words right into my son's mouth. I never said I didn't want him to see a psychologist. I was the one trying to get him in to see a psychologist in the first place!

After my son answered a few more questions by the judge, he asked, "Okay. This is your chance—we're going to be talking again, I'm sure, but I'm just worried about right now what I'm going to do today with what's in front of me. So I really need you to be open with me and tell me what you really want and what you're thinking. I need your help."

My son stated, "I just want to see my mom."

The judge then asked him about his relationship with his two younger brothers and his sister. He asked if anything had gone wrong when my son had last visited me, and he said that he had nothing to complain of and that he enjoyed the time there riding his bike around the neighborhood.

Attorney Black asked a very interesting question regarding the second indication, "Did you ever go biking or do anything like that?"

My son answered, "yes."

Funny, because in the second indication I was still under, it said that I would not let him ride his bike. This whole thing was nothing more than a first-class witch hunt.

Attorney Black continued, "When the judge asked you, you said you know your mom needs some help, right? What do you think she needs help with? You said you don't think that she can control what she does or doesn't know that she's doing it?"

My son said, "I think she needs...help on people skills and stuff like that. I didn't have...too much of a problem with it. Just I guess that she needs a little bit of help. I don't think anything major."

As a registered nurse of 23 years, how could I have ever coped this long without excellent people skills? I was liked and respected at work and in my personal life. I don't blame my son for these statements — he had certainly been coached, and probably would have had to deal with consequences accompanied by a great deal of stress at home if he hadn't said what he was told.

Attorney Black continued, "There are a lot of people that maybe think that a lot of your anxiety has gotten better this Summer. Do you think that's true?"

My son answered, "No. Because of the whole situation. Being separated doesn't help."

Judge Greene excused my oldest son and then brought in my youngest sons, asking them how they were doing and if they were getting along with their older brother. They said that they weren't. He asked them if they missed me and wanted to see me, or if they had any contact with me, and they both agreed that they missed me, would like to see me again, and had not had any contact with me since they got "blocked,"

The attorneys had no questions to ask my sons, so they were dismissed.

The Daughter Is Interviewed

Now, Judge Greene started speaking with my daughter. For the most part, she essentially confirmed what had already been said by Seth and Judith. She insisted that my son's "meltdowns," which she called "inconsolable crying," disappeared as soon as his iPad was taken away, and that the kids were all much happier now. She insisted that I had told my son to send me messages. She insisted, like her father, that her brother was worlds better now and was happier the very day after he cut off contact with me. The usual stuff. And Judge Greene bought it all...hook, line and sinker....or did he?

Conclusion Of The Hearing

Judge Greene came back out onto the bench and said that his conversation with the kids had been very helpful. Judge Greene continued, "So I'm not sure now, given what the children said, that we need to spend a whole lot of time on it, but I do want to look at just some of the messages. Probably—I don't care."

Attorney Black suggested expanding this case to the next day, so the psychologist, who had never shown up, would be able to testify. He insisted that this was part of the reason why they had filed a petition for special relief in the first place and asked Judge Greene if he had looked at the report.

Judge Greene said, "Actually I haven't because I would rely on the testimony. I mean, until it's in, its hearsay."

Attorney Black asked, "I mean, if counsel would stipulate to the entry of the report?" Judge Greene stated, "He is not going to do that."

Judge Greene continued, "I understand your request, Mr. Black, but I'm not sure the psychologist is going to make that big of a difference for our purposes here today. So I want to look at the phone, and then I'm prepared to make a ruling. And then we can talk about a review date after I make my ruling.

"But I think based on—especially after I've heard from the kids, I think I've got a pretty good handle on what's been happening here and how to handle it. Okay?"

I began to realize how inept — and confused — Judge Green really was when his law clerk said, "I didn't know whether you wanted counsel as well?"

Judge Greene said, "No. What do you want me to do?"

The law clerk said, "You see where it has a number and a W? That's how many weeks prior. Scroll all the way up to the top. That's where the history begins. Scroll down to the bottom, and that's most recent, I believe that's how it works."

Judge Greene stated, "For the record, that was my technical expert/law clerk telling me what to do here, although I think I had it figured out."

Judge Greene didn't even know how to use his own computer, let alone what he had done to my family. The emotional abuse my ex-husband would level on the kids would change their lives forever.

Judge Greene stated, "First of all, Miss Petri, Mr. Balor, when you two can't get along and have a dispute and then you bring it to court and ask me to make a decision...I expect my orders to be followed. I don't appreciate either one of you unilaterally disobeying orders, whether it's on the advice of an attorney or not...'"

The judge expressed his disappointment in both of us, but he was especially critical of me, narcissistically saying, "Once again you are your own worst enemy. Your demeanor on the witness stand—you were evasive today, you were vague. You conveniently remember only what you want to remember." Then, he observed, "what saved you today was your children's testimonies." Because my son was so adamant that he wanted to see me in the chamber, and that he had initiated some of the contact, that he would be permitted to visit me. Seth would still have full custody, but they would be allowed to visit every other weekend from Friday after school until Sunday evening.

Then, Judge Greene added in a demeaning tone, "But I'm telling you, if there's a problem—I'm not going to let you see them forever. Okay?... You have got to get it through your head that you need help, and you can't be doing what you want or, 'sticking up for yourself' because you think it's the right thing to do!"

Judith was outright screaming and yelling, infuriated that I would have my sons at all, even if it was just every other weekend unsupervised. My attorney chuckled, leaned over, and told me that this had never been done under indications like mine in court before, and that it was a miracle.

Judge Greene continued to berate me, "You come into court. You expect me to make a decision. I have. And I think I've bent over backwards to be fair to you and to treat you with respect and courtesy. I've made it clear on several occasions I have no interest in keeping you from your kids. And every time I want to give you more, you do something to make me pause and hesitate. And until your son came and talked to me today, I wasn't going to do what I just did. Do you understand me?"

Judge Greene continued his tirade, "Mr. Petri, I know you love your kids too, and they're quite happy with you, but they love their mother regardless of her problems." Yikes! He had just called my ex-husband by my last name; I was beginning to wonder how good Judge Greene's health was, and if he was qualified to be on any case, let alone ours.

Judge Greene also said that I would be allowed to attend school activities, and though Attorney Black tried to argue against it, the judge did not entertain his arguments.

Judge Greene also appeared to have no idea what Parental Alienation is.

"I don't think that I'm going wild and crazy here by giving her one weekend every other month to start." Judge Green said.

Attorney Black asked, "Does this involve the three kids?"

Judge Greene bristled and answered, "Yeah, involves the three kids. Do you have questions?"

Seth asked, "You just said one week every other month. You meant every other weekend?"

Judge Greene, irritated, raised his voice, saying, "The weekend, every other weekend, right. All right?" Then went on to scold Seth by saying, "You need to have your psychological evaluation done in two months. So you need to be evaluated by then. Okay? I don't care who by."

Judge Greene then turned back to me and said in a demeaning tone, "So Ms. Petri, I'm going to leave it to you to pick them up. You're to stay in the car. Okay? You're to be on time, and they can come out and get in your car. Okay? And then you bring them back. I don't think that's unduly burdensome because you don't live that far apart from each other. I just think you two should stay away from each other for a while and not have any contact. That minimizes the potential for trouble. All right? Do you have any other questions?"

There was a question I dared not ask. I wondered why my daughter, nine months later, wanted her clothing all of the sudden. Why not two weeks after her leaving? Teenagers want their clothing and none of this made sense.

I was now a non-custodial parent. Though I was grateful to have some time with the kids, however small, I had no idea how much trouble this would cause me in the future.

A Family Reunited

That afternoon at about 5:00 p.m., my oldest son came to my home after school and rang the doorbell. I smiled and ran to answer the door. Upon opening it, he rushed in, wrapped his arms around me and hugged me tightly. I told him how much I loved him, and he replied that he loved me too. He then went to get a bin of his sister's things and took it out to his father's vehicle. (Seth did comply with the judge's order this time.)

I had accepted long ago that my daughter would not be returning. I have to admit, I was okay with that. The house was calm during the times I had my sons; it was peaceful with normal every day issues. But now that I was a non-custodial parent, I was good enough to have my sons on the weekends, but was otherwise a dead-beat parent. How our lives had changed!

In the meantime, Seth came up with his own idea to let only my mother and husband contact the children via texting. However, my parents being as old as they were did not know how to text, so the grandparents still had no contact.

Then I received an unexpected phone call. Judge Greene had passed away. Linda and I were at the mall when we heard the news. "Praise You, Jesus!" I shouted, staring at the phone. Perhaps I would get a second shot at getting my kids back after all.

Looking back, I wonder if Judge Greene's health had already begun to decline when he made his ruling on my case. When he so intrusively asked me what medications I was on, I should have asked him what was he taking and if that could affect how the hearing would go! When Judge Greene said, "I don't know how to do this," and called my sons by the wrong names, let alone calling my ex-husband by my last name, I seriously question if he was on some type of medication that was interfering with his ability to make sensible decisions on the bench. These poor decisions affected my whole family and potentially my sons' emotional wellbeing for the rest of their lives. This we may never know. But what I do know is that we were not the only family affected by his destructive and biased rulings.

A bizarre incident happened at my son's birthday party. He had several friends over and as we were singing Happy Birthday to him, he blurted out and yelled, "I hate my dad's big fat ugly attorney, and I'm so glad Judge Greene is dead!" I sat back and wished I had that on video. Brad missed it all because he was working out of town at the time. We just continued the party as if nothing had been said, and I began to cut the cake.

 **TAKEAWAY:**

The judge was in collusion with the opposing attorney, that was blatantly clear. He himself had a Narcissistic Personality Disorder along with the opposing counsel and client. "God help us!" I thought. Only seeing the boys every other weekend gives the alienating parent time to work on the children. It doesn't allow the kids time away from the alienator to breathe, relax and form their own opinions; they can't do that when they are being brainwashed.

Lies Breaking Family Ties

Maryann Petri

My Kids sit back and listen
To lies getting in their system,
They hear it and they see it
Then they gradually believe it

Every false allegation is all about me
Accusations too numerous to count you see,
Continuous lies and deceit withstood
If I could change them back I would

Time has lapsed another year goes by
Memories have changed and so have I,
In their minds I do not exist
Countless lies though still persist

Lies cannot stop I'm falling into a pit
Those filthy liars are a piece of shit,
Desperately trying to talk sense into them
But everyone knows where those lies stem

Conflicted yet loyal to their Alienator
Treating my children like a capital expenditure,
Now I sit back and listen to more of the lies
Swiftly cutting what was left of my family ties

PART FOUR:
Was It Really A Broken Heart?

The Non-Custodial Parent's Nightmare

What It Felt Like To Be A Non-Custodial Parent

When I became a non-custodial parent, my world changed forever. Once, I dropped off my oldest son to pick up some things. When I opened the garage door, he came in and embraced me with tears in his eyes. "I missed hearing your voices changing!" I said. I felt like I had missed out on so much in just a few months' time.

I tried to carry on the routine as we did before CPS and Family Court entered and promptly obliterated our lives. The kids would have friends stay over, and one of my oldest son's friends said to him, "You're old enough to pick where you want to live." My son didn't know what to say. He really did make that decision, and told the judge, but the judge ignored it several times when speaking with him. His friend continued to say, "I wish my mom fought for me like your mom fought for you." I explained to his friend not to hold that against his mother because there are a lot of factors that play into the Family Court System. Indeed, I was representing myself, but on an uphill battle with a shield but no sword.

Life As A Non-Custodial Parent

My greatest fear as a non-custodial parent was not knowing if my children were safe. Would they be suffering in an emergency room, and I wouldn't know it, or worse yet, hear about it from a friend the next day?

Seth would never tell me about when and where doctor's appointments were; I was always the last to know. I never knew what vaccines they were getting and had no input into their care. I always told my sons to call me if they were going to the emergency room because I would never know what was going on. For instance, when my youngest son broke his leg in gym class at the middle-school, a friend had called me from the school to let me know that he was being driven to the emergency room, but I didn't know which hospital. It was hopeless.

When it came time to have his cast off, for once I was aware of where he was going and the time. But I had a gut-feeling that was not the correct time. Luckily, Brad was home and I told him, "We have to go now." He replied, "but the appointment isn't until 4:30 p.m." I said, "I have a feeling." The snow was starting to fall lightly to the ground as we drove in.

When we arrived where the orthopedic doctor's office was, there I saw my youngest son standing in front of the building with snow falling down on him. He had been balancing on crutches with his coat open while his father parked the car.

I got out of the car while Brad parked and told my son I would walk him into the lobby. There, I waited for Brad and Seth to come in. We rode the elevator up while I made light conversation. We came into the office and let the receptionist know we were there. When his name was called, Seth and I got up and walked with him into the room to get his cast taken off. I took pictures and made it a light-hearted and happy experience for him. Afterwards, we all left together, and I hugged my son goodbye while I zipped up his winter coat. I glanced at Brad, and he gave me the look that conveyed he recognized that I knew the time of the appointment wasn't right, and he was astonished. I just knew.

As I saw the cast coming off, I noticed that the stepmother wrote, "Kiss, kiss- love Mom." She also underlined it twice. Unbelievable. I was shocked and hurt, but did not make a scene. I said nothing to my son. I just let it go.

When my kids came to stay with me every other weekend, Brad drove home on the weekends from the place he was renting from. We would take them places; new movies that had come out. Things got a little bit better when the child support payment dropped, which was a big help, but not by much as Brad was making the payments on top of lawyer fees. We were trying to do things, take them places, and we both found it stressful as my income as a nurse was now gone.

The kids brought over their X-box's that would later turn into PlayStations. Brad loved to play the games with them. It was very loud in the house and light-hearted hearing a battle going on and the boys (now my "four kids") all yelling and laughing at a PlayStation game. They enjoyed that time together over the weekends until Brad had to drive back to work Sunday at 4:00 p.m.

The kids and I would put on a movie. My oldest son's favorite movies was *The Patriot* and *The Judge*. At first I didn't want to see *The Judge*. I had about enough of judges in my life, but this movie proved to be full of family dynamics. It was excellent as we watched it multiple times and ended up crying together at the end. My youngest liked the *Fast and Furious* movies and *Spiderman*. We would always put in a DVD action movie after Brad left and we had two precious hours left together.

At the end of the weekend they would pack up their things and hug their pets for a long time. I remember my boys weeping as they hugged me by the car in the garage. Even their older brother came over and hugged me very tight. Then we all climbed in the car and, as I drove them back to their father's, we all held on to each other's hands. It was an emotional time. When I dropped them off at their father's house, we hugged in the driveway and there were more tears.

Parental Alienation did not just ruin my life; it ruined the lives of my children. Slowly, I watched my kids go from happy and joyful to anxious, confused, and bitter. Their sweet memories of their early childhood were erased and replaced with lies created by Seth and Judith.

The false allegations and indications brought on by CPS affected my children deeply. Rumors were spread and some of their classmates even taunted them about what happened. Their once happy, carefree faces were now filled with heaviness from the lies and abuse they had been burdened with. They constantly felt a need to defend me, whether at school or at home, and this positively exhausted them. If CPS had done the right thing, all of this anxiety and suffering could have been avoided, and they might have been able to enjoy their childhood and their friends. But that was not our reality.

The Non-Custodial Parent's Fear

Maryann Petri

What do we do about this ill content
From Family Court our bodies are spent,
Paying out fees and hands have been tied
You look at your living child treated as if died

Family Court is a battleground aided by CPS
You are now a Target-parent and under duress,
Your children have been taken away and have no clue
Looking for your car at school and waiting for you

How sad it is for them to finally find out
That you are no longer anywhere about,
They wonder when will they see you next
Only to find themselves in a toxic vortex

Non-custodial Parent please do beware
In due time your child will not care,
And grow to despise you and has taken the bait
For the child you used to know has learned to hate

Life for you all will be grueling and grim
Contacting your child as you go out on a limb,
Breaking a Court Order just to make contact
To make sure your child's life is intact

In time slowly they turn them against you
Sit, Wait and watch there's nothing you can do,
Your child is being groomed to live in fear
But there's a Court Order you all must adhere

A 21st Century Debtor's Prison

Becoming A Pro Se

I was faced with going Pro Se, which means that you become your own attorney "acting one's own behalf." At the time I was tapped out with attorney fees of $30,000. I had had enough, so I took the bull by the horns. I knew my case better than any other attorney around. So, I decided to go it alone and personally explain the case to the judge at every hearing. It was clear – a hard push was needed in order to get my children back to their wishes of a 50-50 shared custody. A lot of finagling was required to get the child support issue resolved. Also, my income was unfairly set at an unrealistic number which inflated the arrears. This was done with full knowledge that my job had ended. Those issues would haunt me for over two years.

To be honest, it was unnerving and stressful gathering the paperwork needed to put motions together. But, along the way, I had gotten a lot of helpful information from other attorneys on YouTube, such as, making four copies of all paperwork and keeping two copies in my file.

I confidently walked into every courtroom conservatively dressed with my head held high. It was important to show no fear, almost to the point of annoying the judge. Speaking the truth was challenging to the judge's authority, and I was threatened with jail.

They all called me crazy, and I often wondered why, until someone explained to me that when a Pro Se does very well in the courtroom, they don't like it. When you handle yourself professionally, and you know your case, they despise you for it. According to Dr. Mark Roseman, "Those litigants who elect to represent themselves 'Pro Se' are frequently viewed by opposing counsel and, indeed, the presiding judge, as impediments to the court process. But often, the Pro Se party is the one who could not afford to continue with a contracted attorney or who believes that results would be no better with an attorney on his or her payroll."

Though I knew the custody case was completely rigged to begin with, there was nothing I could do. The cards were stacked against me in furthering their goal to erase me from my kids' lives. I could've walked in there with a high-powered attorney and I still would have lost. Times like this will happen, but there will be other victories that will take place outside the courtroom. For example, when I was leaving a contempt conference, the opposing attorney stated to someone, as he walked four paces behind me, "I hate her, she argues like my ex-wife." Upon hearing that statement, I was completely elated and walked on cloud nine for over a year. To compare me to her was a backhanded compliment that I will never forget. Those are the small victories you might encounter.

There will be major victories, and yes, it's stressful. Going into a courtroom with a biased judge and an incompetent attorney is not helpful to anyone's self-esteem. But know this: they cannot break you when you keep coming back. I won the child support case in Superior Court. The verdict was vacated and remanded, which lowered the child support from $1,000 a month down to $180.

I did not give up; I just kept appealing to Superior Court. Every time I appealed, they would send more instructions and make more demands, and insisted I do it right on the time deadline needed for providing those briefs and reproduced records. These demands stated how many briefs and reproduced records they would need, and how many opposing counsels needed, etc. I submitted everything they asked for. In the end, I didn't have the opportunity to go in and argue; it was actually a very quiet victory notice I received in the mail five months later, but only after having been thrown into "debtor's prison" for non-payment and having literally suffered a heart attack.

The key to succcss is being steadfast in your desire to go on and continue, even when things aren't looking good. The Superior Court was a win that literally saved my life and totally changed the game, even though my children were aging out.

A major victory will actually put the opposing attorney on the defense for once. It's rare that a Pro Se wins and is definitely something to celebrate and be proud of. Two wins in Superior Court (I also won a ruling on a pension fund a few years prior), are a better track record than most attorneys have.

There are times when I look back and wonder how I got through it all. I was called crazy and belittled in a courtroom full of people. I'm sure they wondered in the back of their minds why they hadn't broken me. I would not allow that to happen. I would not let them conquer me. To this day, at least, I can say I did argue very well and won a major case.

Pro Se Courtroom Story

I stood at the rail before Judge Speer, who was always in a bad mood, next to Attorney Black and Seth. I tried not to yawn and shake my head in disbelief through Attorney Black's pontification of long drawn out lies and half-truths. A poker face is one thing a Pro Se has to maintain at all times. A Pro Se has to act like nothing upsets him just like an attorney does. That's another thing an attorney taught me. One example is when opposing Attorney Black stated, "I requested that she notify all her physicians and have them here, and none of them are present, your Honor."

When it was my turn to speak, I enjoyed using Attorney Black's theatrical arm gestures in such bravado that would be enough to make anyone think I was Evita Peron. Ironically, it was he that taught me to do this. I would watch him throughout the hearings and apparently this is how he operated, so I began by using the same motions. I raised my arms and waved them around mimicking Attorney Black and replied, "Your Honor, Attorney Black only gave me less than 48 hours' notice to have all my physicians here, and if he wanted them here, perhaps he should have subpoenaed them himself. Also, if Attorney Black thinks I am so competent to be a registered nurse, then perhaps we should immediately go back to 50-50 custody."

It was silent in the courtroom. The judge nodded her head in agreement. I was pleased as I glanced over to Attorney Black. The look on his face was priceless; he was stone still looking very angry. I put a half smile on my face as usual and pivoted, walking away from the rail and out of the courtroom with my father.

After that hearing, I did notice a change in Attorney Black. When I was speaking at the rail, out of the corner of his eye I could see he was watching me using his arm gestures. After that, he stopped behaving with his arms flailing and kept them to his side.

Really, the judge said nothing much after that, and we were excused.

All we had to do was wait for the judgment in the mail. I began to fear the mailbox years ago. Most of the time her judgments arrived the next day, which I found very suspicious... she had this already wrapped up yesterday.

When I did get the judgment, it was the usual order like the last order, that I was to pay the full amount of child support, and I still owed thousands in the arrears known as back support.

She knew I was not allowed to work as a nurse, as I would be around children due to the indications. It amazes me that she completely disregarded the Child Protective Services Law where one cannot work anywhere where children would be around. But she did not care, she wanted that child support paid with Title IV-D attached for her pleasure.

Again, I have to reiterate that victory will come at times when you represent yourself.

Pro Se's Don't Have To Pay A Dime

Linda and I drove well over three hours to get to the Superior Court. We came in to the room where the lawyers signed in, and I was number 14 on the list. There was a gentleman sitting there in the room by himself, and he told me that they never see a "lone female" arguing for a case like mine. "You have a lot of...." He said, trailing off.

"Balls, right?" I asked. We both laughed.

I figured we would be out of there by noon, but it was already 1:45 pm by the time I was called to argue. I was given only 15 minutes to speak and 5 minutes of rebuttal time. Attorney Black was there to argue for Seth. So, once again, I mimicked him, by raising my hands and throwing back my head exactly as he would. He was never that dramatic around me again.

When I finished, the judge who was once again not in a good mood folded his arms and leaned forward into the microphone, "So Pro Se's don't have to pay a dime."

I stared at him, stunned. Several months ago, I had put a few funny quips about lawyers and judges on my YouTube channel. In one skit, I had explained the role of a Pro Se and said, "But a Pro Se doesn't have to pay one dime." I hadn't realized until then just how closely these people were watching me.

Attorney Black finished what he had to say, and we were dismissed. I knew I had lost the case, but I tried to pretend that it didn't bother me. As we left the building, the elevators were running slow, and I insisted that we get into the elevator with Attorney Black. Linda looked at me like she thought I was crazy. When we stood with him, I acted as if I didn't have a care in the world, laughing and joking with Linda. We all left together, and I saw where Attorney Black parked his vehicle — in the $25.00 per hour parking lot. What a joke. This was just another way to rack up attorney fees for his client.

Of course, I did lose the case, so my child support case would have to be ruled on by a lower court. Little did I know how badly this next case could go.

Judge Speer asked my position, and I explained the situation. Attorney Black said that I had voluntarily left my job implying that I could work as a nurse if I wanted, and Judge Speer admitted it as evidence.

At the end of Spring, I was back again in front of Judge Speer. One of my co-workers, who had gone before this judge, herself, told me that the color of her lipstick — whether it was peach or light-pink — was a good indicator as to how she would rule. She was wearing pink, the color to be feared. Eventually, Judge Speer decided to defer all of our motions to the Superior Court.

Realizing Jail Is A Possibility

In the meantime, I was required to go to Contempt Conferences. They wanted to know why I wasn't paying an impossible amount of child support of $1,00.00 a month plus $96.00 on arrears. I was still suspended from my nursing job, and the only sort of work I could get were small, minimum wage jobs. Yet, they were still calculating my child support at a nurse's salary. My arrears were set at $2,568.42, and were due in full — IMMEDIATELY. I was going to have to take this all the way to the Superior Court to get anything done, and this time I couldn't even afford an attorney to help me.

The young man who sat down with me shuffled through the paperwork and said, "I just want you to know that this is all BS." He asked if I had $700.00 to give to Domestic Relations; I told him that I was now working a minimum-wage job and the best I could offer was $75.00. He told me where to take the money and to get a receipt. Then he said that if this continues, there will be contempt hearings, and I may eventually be imprisoned for non-support. I literally felt my bladder loosen and thought I might wet my pants right there in his office.

In January, I had a dream that I went to prison. I didn't think too much of it at the time, even though I was awaiting the outcome of a child support case sitting at Superior Court. Little did I know that was the first of many warnings.

The other dream I had was three years prior, where I was at church with my three-month-old son who was sleeping on the front pew. I saw Judith come through the side entrance, staring at my baby. She would not take her eyes off him as she continued walking. When I woke up, I was so anxious, it took me a long time to get back to sleep.

The boys wanted to return to 50/50 custody, and asked me if I could do anything. They said that they would happily stand on the witness stand for me.

So, I went to the Conciliatory Office of the courthouse and scheduled a conference for early that Fall. Seth did not show up for this important conference, but his attorney did. I argued that my sons were not safe or well taken care of by Seth. I showed them how my youngest children had to make their own birthday invitations and were required to ride their bikes to and from soccer practice on a dangerous road where two deaths had taken place within the last three months. I had e-mailed Seth explaining my concerns for their safety and even offered to drive to and from soccer practice, but Seth refused. I also made it clear that I was doing this at our kid's request.

Attorney Black stood up quickly, shouting, "I've had about enough of this ridiculousness!" He slammed his briefcase on the table, put his coat back on, and walked out the door.

In less than a week, I received a formal letter in the mail that a new custody trial was ordered. I couldn't believe it! Something had finally gone my way. When I saw the boys the following weekend, they were thrilled to hear the news.

Sham Of A Hearing

When the day of the hearing came, I was full of hope. Sadly, things would not turn out the way I wanted. Though we had a new judge, this one was a very close acquaintance of Attorney Black as well.

I subpoenaed several witnesses — my parents, close friends and my sons — as they had requested of me. But when the day finally came, my sons were nowhere to be found.

I sat at my side of the courtroom and Attorney Black handed me paperwork that I already had. The judge came out on the bench. With him, Judge Cain L. Grey had every document from our case, which was now nearly two feet thick.

The judge stated, "the reason we were here is for a petition for special relief, which has already been ruled on by Judge Greene." The judge said that this case was similar to ones that had already been before the court, and that Judge Greene had ordered that no more of these petitions should be made without permission.

I couldn't believe what I was hearing. I thought we were here for a custody trial — that is what was ordered, after all — and Attorney Black had turned it into a petition for special relief? I had never even heard Judge Greene say that I could no longer file petitions for special relief without permission, but that wasn't even what we were here for. There was no jury present, and I already knew that this "case" was going to make a mockery of the law.

Judge Grey continued listing more reasons why I had no right to appeal this case in the first place, including fees that I was apparently required to make during any counseling hearings which I was not able to make. In the end, he concluded, "Therefore, it is my reason and legal conclusion that this trial is improperly brought before the court at this time and the proceedings must and should be quashed... therefore, this court is adjourned."

With that being said, Judge Grey got up, picked up the file, and walked off the bench. As he was leaving, I called out, "Your Honor, my children are being neglected!" He didn't do so much as turn around to acknowledge me.

This was an ambush of another kind. I took Attorney Black's papers and lightly tossed them on his desk. Seth, standing only two feet away from his attorney, meekly asked, "Did she try to throw those papers at me?"

I picked up my sons that afternoon. When they got into the SUV, they asked, "Mom, was there court today?" I told them, "yes there was court this morning and grandma and grandpa were there along with several other witnesses." My son reported that in the morning their father told them it was cancelled. Seth had lied to his own children.

These Contempt Hearings and Contempt Conferences were starting to take a physical and emotional toll on me. In late Spring, things were way out of control. Judge Speer still based my income capability at $3,522.47 and Seth's income at $4,820.30, and he deliberately inflated my arrears to $16,248.80. I wondered if I would ever be free of this fabricated debt.

There were Support/Contempt hearings twice a month since the previous year. I didn't know what to think of the one that took place during Holy Week. I was directed to sit in the contempt box with at least 14 men, two of whom were in scrubs and shackled at the wrists and ankles. Seth had come with his parents in tow. The bailiff walked over to Attorney Black and asked abrasively, "What are you doing here?"

Attorney Black leaned over the pew and replied, "We're just here to observe."

Yes, observe Judge Speer sending me to jail on Easter week — all for inflated child support and arrears that I could never pay and should never have owed! Linda sat with me in the pews, and I could tell that she was worried, too. When Judge Speer entered, she called me up to testify first.

Leaving the contempt box, I touched each man on the shoulder and whispered, "Bless you." I then approached the railing and stood by the Domestic Relations attorney, listening to Judge Speer.

Judge Speer said that unless I could come up with $2,000 to go towards child support and arrears, I would have to go to prison for the next two months. I would have one month to do so.

Seth walked quickly up to the railing and announced, without even addressing Judge Speer, "I think the court record is very, very clear on this matter. Since day one she has defied numerous court requests, whether it's custody or support. This has been going on for five years. She's not working. Plus, because she is being defiant of the custody order, she's trying to make as little as she can just to get out of the court order, and that's the way it's been."

Defiant in what custody order? Prove it. He didn't have anything to back up what he was saying. The reason I wasn't working was self-explanatory due to the Child Protective Laws.

Taking my kids away was not enough, I saw that now. His true goal, whether it was in the beginning or not, was to send me to prison so that my children would never see me again. To exact revenge on me, perhaps, for divorcing him so many years ago. And it almost worked.

It was unreal. I personally would not have done this to him because of what it would do to my children. Not only that, I couldn't believe his parents could be a party to all of this. I looked over at his mother and there she sat, glaring at me. Judge Speer stated, "All right. I understand what the issues are...I am going to find Ms. Petri in contempt of court for failing to pay her support. Ms. Petri, I'm going to give you 30 days from today's date in which to make a payment in the amount of $2,000.00. We will accept the pension funds, if you can get them released, and we will apply that. If not, that purge amount will stand. And if you fail to pay that, I'll incarcerate you for a period of two months and establish a purge in the amount of $2,000.00. And I'll authorize you for work release, if you were to qualify. All right. Thank you very much, everyone. Thank you."

"You need to understand something." Linda said, pulling me aside. "Seth Balor wants you in jail to 'pay' for what you've done to him, and teach you a lesson, and he's just using the support case as a means to do so. He has no respect for you whatsoever."

I could not produce the $2,000.00 Judge Speer demanded. Judge Speer must have had something against me. As I have said earlier, for the past two years, she had continuously estimated my salary at the level of a registered nurse, ignoring my physician's orders and verification forms. My arrears were at approximately $16,248.80, and she increased it another $2,000 for no apparent reason. Between the Contempt Conferences and the hearings, I felt powerless to stop her. It was a level of harassment I had never been exposed to. Linda and I concluded that Judge Speer was on a high-paid power-trip.

Sent To Prison

Here is some data collected in the year of 2019: 500 non-support warrants were issued and $38,000.00 collected in relation to the 500 warrants. This is in regards to all parents in general. There are parents who collect money under the table and do not report their incomes, and there are others that file false allegations or continue court hearings so that a parent loses their job due to continued court appearances.

I showed up at the Sheriff's office at 11:00 a.m., the day after Mother's Day, and turned myself in. I took several Clonopin, one of my prescribed medications, with me, as I was warned that they withhold medications in prison. I then followed about twelve men towards a transport vehicle. A metal divider separated the male prisoners from the female prisoners and those who transported the vehicle. I was feeling dizzy and nauseated, so the sheriff had to help me off the transport vehicle and into the building. I had a hard time believing this was really happening.

When we arrived, I was handcuffed to a bar, and a guard came to speak with me. "Do you have any scars?" he asked. I slipped my left hand out of the cuff and said, "I have a small scar here."

The guard's eyes widened. "Somebody come and tighten her cuffs!" he said. After asking me a few more questions, he asked, "And are you ambidextrous?" I slid my dominant hand out of my cuff to show him, and this time the guard started laughing, "I should've expected you to do that!" he said.

Once the questions ended, I was placed in a cold, brick holding room. I shivered. If I had known how cold it would be and how long I would be in there, I would've worn more than jeans, a button-down shirt and sandals. I sighed heavily, and my voice echoed across the walls. The room had excellent acoustics. So I started singing—softly, at first—to soothe my nerves and pass the time in that well-lit, empty room.

Four hours passed and the guard swung open the door again, this time with another woman in hand. She had soft blue eyes with a calm and gentle expression. "I'm blessed to meet you," she said. I was surprised by the greeting; that wasn't the sort of comment you'd expect from someone in a holding cell. Then again, I wasn't the sort of hardened criminal you'd expect to be in prison either! We both quietly discussed our situations, and I eventually mentioned how great the acoustics were in the room. She asked me to sing something and cheered when I finished. Then, she asked me to sing another song, and we started singing in harmony together. There was something so peaceful about listening to our voices echo across the holding cell walls. Who knew that you could find beauty in a place as dark as this?

Sometime later, a guard came into the holding cell and said, "It's so nice to hear singing in here instead of yelling." He offered me my free phone call, and I called Brad. I didn't talk for too long; I just let him know I was okay, and I loved him.

At around 7:30 a.m. a guard brought me out of the holding cell and took me to the nurse. She spoke in a calm, pleasant manner, asking about my medical history. I explained that I have occasional bouts of hypoglycemia and mentioned the medications that I take. When she asked to take my blood pressure, I slid my right hand out of the cuff — the guards still hadn't put it on tight enough! This didn't appear to bother the nurse, and after she took my blood pressure, I started to put my hand back into the cuff. Before I could, a tall guard with bleached hair came in and started yelling at me. He threatened to put me in, "E-5," whatever that was, and threatened me during my entire walk back to the holding cell.

"Don't you talk to me like that," I said. "I'm a registered nurse, and I'm not putting up with your attitude."

At about 3:00 a.m., a female guard came to take me to my cell.

"Goodbye!" I said to my newfound friend. We had become friends in the most unusual of circumstances, but now I wasn't sure if I would ever see her again.

The guard marched me into the jail, and we passed cell after cell until we finally reached mine. The door squeaked as it swung open, and the guard motioned me inside. "Cellie, you have someone to share your cell," she said.

I walked inside, setting down the small bin and all that I was allowed to keep, that had been assigned to me — which had a small toothbrush, toothpaste, soap, and a cup. After I shuffled around for a few minutes, trying to comprehend this small room that was supposed to be "home" for the next few months, my cellmate whispered sternly, "Just go to bed!"

I had only slept for a few hours when they announced on a loudspeaker that it was time for breakfast. It was Tuesday morning. My cellmate, now in a better mood, told me the do's and don't's of prison. "Stay behind the white lines surrounding the guards areas," she said, "that's the quickest way to get in trouble around here."

"Thanks." I said.

When my cellie and I left our cell, and I grabbed my tray and got in line in the cafeteria. It wasn't a terrible meal, really, and there was so much food that I didn't think I would eat all of it.

"Can I have some of that when you're done, please?" A woman, much younger than me asked sheepishly.

"Sure, go ahead," I said.

"The hungry ones are the heroin addicts," a women told me, "withdrawals are hell, and you get so hungry it feels like your stomach is eating your insides while you're going through them."

Soon, the nurse came to deliver medications. I got in line with everyone else and when it was my turn, I said, "Do you have everything for me?"

The nurse shuffled through her paperwork and found my name, "You're on the list," she said, "but it's going to take about two days. We need to talk to your physician first.

"Two days?" I said in disbelief, raising my voice. "I don't have two days! Do you know what sort of withdrawals I could go into by then? I need my morning medication now. Some of the withdrawals from these medications could kill me." I told her I was especially concerned about the Lamictal, because if you don't take it regularly, you could develop a rash that would lead to death. I also needed my Wellbutrin and Clonopin, and quickly.

"Gee, what else do you take?" the nurse ask disinterestedly, clearly not concerned about how this would affect me.

"I take Seroquel to help me sleep at night," I said.

The nurses eyes widened, and she literally jumped back at her desk, "You're on Seroquel?" she asked, "Are you psychotic?"

I could feel my face flushing, I was so humiliated. How positively degrading of her! She must've been straight out of nursing school to be so ignorant about the uses of that drug. "No, it's prescribed to help me sleep," I insisted, "Even my pharmacist takes it for that."

The nurse straightened and pursed her lips together. "Oh-" she said, "Well, I'll take a note of it. There's nothing else we can do for you today, so I'll have to ask you to leave."

And back to the cells we went. Once we were inside, the prisoners who had committed more serious crimes, like murder, came out to eat. Once they were done, we were let out for socialization. I sat at the metal picnic table with the others and put my head in my hands. The dizziness and nausea from my missed dose of medications were already starting to set in.

One young woman piqued my attention when she said, "I had Attorney Black. He was only with me for one hearing and then he never returned my calls."

"It's disgusting, isn't it?" I said, "they take your retaining fee, show up once or twice, and then drop you just because they can."

Another younger woman in the group had just come back from a hearing with Judge Glass. "He yelled at my mother because I'm addicted to heroin, and then he sentenced me to six more months in this place! Why would he do that?"

Several of the inmates asked about what happened to me, and I shared with them my story. One very young woman, approximately 19 years old, approached and said, "We know you don't do heroin because you have really good skin." I thanked her and said I wouldn't have the slightest clue where to get it.

Another woman who was somewhere in her 60s told us, "All I am is a mother who got caught with drugs, and I've been put through hell ever since." She was so gentle and kind, telling us captivating stories from the news and her own personal life that had us all laughing.

Prison was nothing like I expected. These weren't hardened criminals; they were drug addicts, at the worst, and, in the case of about 40% of the women, people with child support non-compliance. Very few that I met seemed like people who deserved to be in jail.

Late afternoon on Tuesday, I heard over the intercom the guard shout, "Move!"

"What's going on?" I asked.

"It's phone time." Cellie said.

We all rushed to the telephones that were placed in groups of four throughout the general area. I grabbed a phone and was given a series of numbers that had to be input first, but I couldn't read them without my glasses. I went to the guards and stood behind the white line, waiting to be acknowledged.

"What is it?" the guard asked, motioning me forward.

"Could you please write these numbers a little bigger for me, so I can see them? I didn't bring my readers with me."

"Whatever." The guard said, rolling her eyes. She slipped the paper out from under my fingertips, wrote out the numbers, and walked away from me, as if I had asked her to do some absurdly difficult task.

That afternoon, I chose to stay in my cell. The nausea and dizziness from withdrawals began to be too much. I started noticing a dull pain in my chest as well, but tried to ignore it.

My stomach turned when I smelled the rancid meal prepared for dinner. It was two hotdogs sitting on what looked like slimy oatmeal. I stared at my meal forlornly, and when it became clear I wasn't going to eat them, one of the inmates asked if she could have them. When I said yes, she was actually grateful! How sad that she would be grateful for something like that.

Later that evening, medications were once again distributed. "Name?" the nurse asked. "Maryann Petri," I said.

The nurse shuffled through her paperwork and said, "There's nothing here for you."

My stomach fell. I didn't know how much longer I could handle this! "I need my medicine." I said, "I haven't taken anything since Monday morning, and the withdrawals are killing me."

"Well, what are your medications?" she said.

"Clonopin, Lamictal, Wellbutrin and Seroquel," I said.

"Oh, they all want Clonopin," a guard beside me said in a patronizing tone.

"No, you don't understand," I said, "I'm starting to have chest pain, and I'm diaphoretic, and I have back pain by my shoulder blade. I think I need to go to the ER; this just isn't safe."

"Oh, we don't do that here." The guard said.

In the end, the only thing the nurse gave me was some Pepto-Bismol for nausea. This had to be some sort of human rights violation! When I returned to my cell, I laid down on my bed and whispered, "Please, God, don't let me die here!"

Life And Injustices In Prison

I could hardly sleep at night — the female night guards made sure of that — so most of the sleep I got came during the day. They kept everyone up with loud, obnoxious conversations, and I began to wonder if they actually enjoyed keeping us sleep deprived. That Wednesday evening, the nurse gave me Librium and Pepto-Bismol. "We'll get your full dose to you by Saturday," she said.

As soon as I sat down after taking Pepto-Bismol while holding my cup, I projectile-vomited. I held the cup up to my mouth, trying to contain the puke, and ran to my cell so I could throw up in the toilet. Unfortunately, the cell door was closed, and I collapsed to my hands and knees, throwing up in the floor of the cafeteria instead.

"Someone let her in, please!" one of the inmates shouted. A tall, female guard slid the door open and stared at me emptily.

"You do know I'm not a heroin addict?" I asked.

"I know" the guard said, her voice flat and devoid of emotion. Then, she turned away and shouted at one of the inmates, "Clean this up, already. I found the Librium pill!"

After that, the guards believed that I really was going through withdrawals. "Petri, do you want to take a shower?" a guard asked over the intercom. I accepted, grateful for the opportunity to change into fresh scrubs and clean myself up. Once I was done, a guard walked me back to my cell and told my cellmate, "Keep a close eye on her, okay?" But I knew that wasn't going to happen; she just threw the covers over her head and went to sleep.

By Thursday morning, I was on an all-liquid diet. As I drank out of my mug, a few of the inmates asked how I was doing. One even added, "I was praying for you last night!" I tried to smile and thanked them, but inside I was falling apart. I was horrified for my future. After breakfast, a nice, young inmate sat beside me and said, "Dude, you can do this! I was on the same stuff, and I got through it." However she was the approximate age of 20.

"Petri, to the office!" a voice shouted. I looked up and a female guard directed me to where I should go, shouting at me to hurry. I knocked on the door to the office where a young man sat at his desk, shuffling through paperwork. He looked up and motioned me inside. "I'm not used to people with manners," he said. Then, he added, "Judge Speer has you eligible for work release. Is that something you're interested in?"

"Not without my medication," I said, explaining my situation and the symptoms I was experiencing.

The man dismissed my concerns and continued to inform me about how work release would go. He even asked if I would be able to drive myself to it. "You want me to drive myself?" I asked in disbelief, "my car isn't here to begin with, and I'm in no position to drive with how dizzy and terrible I'm feeling."

"Oh, that's right." He said, "Well, that's all I need from you then."

I walked away, realizing that if I had said "yes" they would have let me drive to work release in a heartbeat. How could they even consider allowing someone to drive in my condition?

Back at the picnic tables, one inmate brought out pictures of her kids to show us. She said that she hasn't been allowed to see them for four years. As soon as I saw the picture and heard her story, my heart broke as I thought of my own children that had been taken away from me. I burst into tears and ran to my cell.

"Petri, get back out here!" the guard said as I lay down on my bed.

"I'm nauseated; I need to lay down," I said.

Thankfully, the guard allowed me to rest, and I napped for much of the afternoon.

For lunch, I was given a Styrofoam cup full of powder. There were no instructions on how to use it, but I figured it must be some sort of powdered broth. So I brought it back to the cell and mixed a small amount of it with water from my drinking fountain. From the looks of it, it appeared to be beef broth. I dumped the rest of it in the trash.

That afternoon, I received a small dose of Lamictal, Librium and Wellbutrin, as well as the Pepto-Bismol for nausea. My doses were still well below what I needed, and these withdrawals were really starting to take a toll on me. I knew that it wouldn't be safe for me to go on this way much longer, even if my full doses did arrive on Saturday. "I'm going to have to call my father and see if he'll pay for the purge," I said to my cellmate.

"Well, we're all in here for a reason," she said.

I shifted my eyes down to look at her and said in an angry, bitter tone, "Not when you're innocent."

📖 TAKEAWAY:

How did this happen to me? As I would soon learn, I was a victim of the jail-for-profit scam called Domestic Relations, which manufactures "dead-beat" parents through deliberately inflated child support orders. This forces the friends and relatives of the victims to come up with the cash to keep the victim out of jail.

If a judge believes they can get money out of your family, then you become a moving-target-parent. Salary estimations are deliberately put higher than any person can pay, and these judges don't care if your family has to go into debt to pay it. But if you don't have the "connections" to money that the judge thinks you have, as in my case, you get sent to jail. Either way, it's a win for the judge. One way, it makes the money for their friends; the other way, it makes more money for more friends. Of course, none of this is legal, but it happens far more frequently than you'd think. Perhaps unsurprisingly, this usually isn't a problem for anyone working in Domestic Relations, most know how to manipulate the well to their desired, predetermined outcome. They believe that anyone who appears in front of a judge is a scumbag who deserves to be punished. True justice doesn't matter to them.

This was a deliberate calculation on Judge Speer's part — she knew what she was doing — and she knew that she could extract money out of my relatives by putting me into prison. I am not the first person that this has happened to, and unless we do something to change this, it will continue to happen to many more well-meaning parents.

How do illegal activities like this occur unabated? In my opinion, it is due to a lack oversight and accountability in the Domestic Relations Department. A Court Administrator will look the other way and let the judges do whatever they want. He cashes his check and leaves, refusing to say a word to anyone about the corruption involved.

I believe one of the main reasons so many non-compliant parents are imprisoned is a need to fill prisons. A prison needs to maintain an optimal number of inmates to justify its grotesque size. When there weren't enough criminals to meet the necessary quota, they devised a plan to get more people in prison through inflated orders for child support that were impossible for people to pay. When the target ended up short of the required amount, they went to jail. Great idea, right?

Most people go into this naively, wanting to believe there will be justice, but instead of justice, they are robbed blind and taken advantage of. Some lawyers will take a client's money and then intentionally torpedo the case if the judge doesn't like the client. The lawyers get paid no matter how the case goes, but they have to work with the judges every day, and they have learned that it's best to keep them happy.

Judges and lawyers thrive on contentious divorces and custody cases because of the massive income they create. Courts regularly and consistently rule in favor of the unfit parent and prey on the desperate fit parent to keep the parties coming back to court. This is all in the interest of their wallet, not in the best interest of the children. The children are used as pawns to take away as much money from the parents as possible.

The act of using incarceration to willfully deprive any inmate of necessary medical attention was ruled an unconstitutional violation of the 8th Amendment by the U.S. Supreme Court in 1976, because it causes "wanton infliction of pain" upon the victims. Unfortunately, the reality is that this is still a common practice throughout U.S. prisons. If you need your prescription drugs, they will be cut off the minute you set foot in prison. If you bring in your own medications, they will be taken away. In my case, I was on Benzodiazepines, drugs that are incredibly dangerous to go off of cold turkey. Even though it is life threatening, the prison didn't care.

Unlike criminals, child support inmates have no right to a public defender, much less a phone call. If they can't even gather the money to pay for a purge, then how would there be any way to pay a lawyer thousands for a retainer fee at close to $300.00 an hour?

Non-support inmates are convicted without a trial by the same judge that inflated the support in the first place, making them easy targets for the judge's friends, allies, and generous sponsors. Criminals that are imprisoned for a violent crime, in fact, get treated better than non-support inmates.

Originally, this system was designed to persecute black males, who still constitute the largest number of support arrests by far. But now, this system has slowly expanded to just about everyone. There is simply no way to actually know how many whites have received inflated orders; more whites have friends and relatives with money and good credit, so as logic goes, a much smaller percentage of whites with inflated orders actually become incarcerated.

We must fight for accountability within the Family Court, Domestic Relations, and Support-Contempt courts. It is essential that juries be present to ensure fair and just trials. It is an absolute tragedy that so many families have been hurt and broken apart in this way. Children are suffering greatly, and innocent parents are labeled mentally ill and unfit, not because of anything they did, but because of greed, lies, and collusion. These labels will haunt that target-parent not only in Family Court, but in Support Conferences and De Novo Hearings as well.

The Sacrificial Lamb of Non-Support

Maryann Petri

There you sit in Contempt
Looking at your hardworking hands,
But the judge sees something much more
In you, the Title IV-D sacrificial lamb

You work at a job or two as it's the best you can do
Extra hours worked trying to pay their demand for Support,
Only to find the Ex really wants you imprisoned
For revenge from a past action and to tear you apart.

But what happens next is a nightmare
For the Sheriffs take you into prison,
Sitting behind bars for not really a crime
You wonder if the judge ever did long division

For there are others that sit for Non-Support
A purge amount they could not pay,
Sitting around waiting for each month to pass
How does one stand it from day to day

It doesn't matter how hard you have worked
That's not good enough for the judge,
You'll rot in prison until that debt is paid
And miss your children so very much

It is your children who will suffer the most
Their taunting peers all know you're in prison,
Your children stand alone and defenseless
With their hatred for the judge's spiteful decision

Feed Seth Whatever
He Wants

"Move!" a voice shouted over the intercom. I stood at the door, my heart racing at what I was about to do.

"Don't just stand there like a child! Go to the phone!" my cellmate said.

I raced to the phones and just barely beat another prisoner to one of them. My hands shook as I dialed the number for my father. "I've got to get out of here or I'm coming out in a body bag," I told him.

"How can I help you?" my father asked with fear in his voice.

"Please, help me pay the purge," I said. "I'm sure Brad can help with half of it, but I need to get out of here. I'm not getting my medications, and I'm going to come out in a body bag." I said to my 79-year-old father.

"I'll go pay it in the morning," my father said. I also gave him instructions that when he pays it, he shouldn't leave until they fax it to the prison, and then I would be released shortly.

The nurse again gave us our medication. It was the same: Librium, Wellbutrin, a partial dose of Lamictal and Pepto-Bismol.

I was so sleep deprived at this point that I didn't even feel human anymore. I could see how prison uprisings happen. This treatment was beyond inhumane.

It was around 10:30 the next morning when a guard announced my release. The inmates cheered and clapped. I smiled and began to cry. The guard told me to go to the doors near where a set of other guards stood.

I went to another area where a tall, male guard gave me my clothing and showed me where I could change. Afterwards, I signed some forms and went to another door where I hit a buzzer that opened to the outside world. It was a beautiful, sunny day. My father stood there, waiting; I ran and hugged him tightly. "Thank you!" I said.

The two of us walked to the car, and I headed to the back seat to lie down. I didn't have the energy to stand, I was so sick. I told my dad to go get a fish sandwich and a Hi-C drink.

"Is this going to happen again?" my father angrily asked as I wolfed down the sandwich. He was older now, frail, and his eyes showed just how tired and fearful he was of dealing with things like this.

"I'm so sorry," I said, my face flushing with anger at what Seth had put us through, "But unless I can find a way to change things, this will keep happening. Maybe even every three or four months. Apparently, we are going to have to feed Seth whatever he wants or I go to jail."

Around that time, my friend Tina Craig called. My father picked up the phone, and she sounded frantic on the other line. "We're on our way home," he told her, handing me the phone.

"Are you out? Are you okay?" she asked me. She said she would stop by my house in the afternoon to help with the kids for their weekend visit. The first thing I did when I got home was take a shower. It felt so wonderful to get the smell of prison off me. Before I knew it, Tina showed up with a chicken dinner with all the fixings and embraced me in a big hug. "I'm so glad you're okay!" she said.

Tina drove me to Seth's house, and my sons came out to meet me. They hardly spoke a word to me during the drive home, which wasn't too much of a problem since I was so exhausted anyway.

Once they settled into their rooms, I gave them their meals and talked with them for a while. "What was it like in prison?" my oldest son asked. I told him as little about the experience as I could — just that I got sick and Grandpa had to get me out.

"Dad said you'd have a TV and tennis courts and be able to go do things," my oldest son said.

"That's not exactly how it worked," I said, explaining to him the difference between federal and local prisons.

My son said that he had gotten into a fight with his father when he found out I was in prison. When he did so, Seth took him by the back of the neck at one point and threw a full water bottle at him. He then told me that his father sat him down in front of the computer and showed him my mug shot, and that kids had made fun of him for having a mother in prison. I had no power to help them; all I could do was encourage them to speak with a school counselor and offer my love and support.

Maryann's Mug Shot

How could their father lie to his own kids and treat them like that? Whatever love he did have for his kids, it was clear that he hated me much more. Taking the kids was not enough. Seth had to inflict emotional pain, too.

My children endured so much suffering — all for the sake of vengeance using Title IV-D, a law that enforces child support obligations against non-custodial parents, and a vindictive judge.

Two weeks later, I went to Seth's house to pick up my kids for another weekend together. Seth had finally finished landscaping the outside of his home, a project he had been working on for some time. "That's where all grandpa's money went to get me out of prison—" I told my oldest son, "but I still don't see any braces on your teeth!"

Saying Goodbye To My Nursing Career

After leaving prison, I continued to see my physicians and counselor in order to get my life back in control. But this small semblance of control didn't last long. Soon there was another letter in the mail for another contempt conference. This was truly becoming a nightmare that would never end.

My husband, Brad, came home that weekend and said that we would have to sell the house and move to New York for a better contracting job. We talked about putting the house on the market, but I feared that Domestic Relations and Judge Speer would call any profit made off of the house an "income." I told Brad to put the house in his name alone to protect him and everything he worked hard for.

Around 7 p.m. one evening, my husband was in the living room and I just couldn't stand listening to the television anymore, so I went into our bedroom just to lay down in the dark. I stared at the wall. A strange darkness loomed over and consumed me. I didn't know how much longer I could go on with constant threats of going to jail and going before Judge Speer after every Contempt Conference. How much more could I possibly take? I seriously considered that taking an overdose might be the only solution to this situation. But then I considered, as I lay there in the darkness, what would that would do to my children. I lay there for quite a while thinking about my suicide options when another thought struck me: *stay alive and that will irritate the ex.* Despite my temptation to end it all, I felt the pressure to just keep going.

Several weeks later, I sent out my brief and reproduced record for the child support argument to the Superior Court, and yes, the paperwork was just as exhausting as the name sounds. After the court received my paperwork, they sent me a letter stating that there weren't enough judges to listen to the arguments on the schedule, so they would only be reading the briefs. I couldn't believe it! I had prepared a case to argue, and I wanted to do it! I was so disappointed.

Things only got worse when I visited Jen Larson that Summer. She told me that she felt I couldn't be passing medications safely to patients in my condition. Because of all the stress and trauma I had been through, my ability to concentrate had diminished greatly. She was going to contact the state licensing board and recommend that they pull my license as a registered nurse. My career was officially over.

I walked slowly away from her office, feeling distraught and hopeless. I was nothing now. Nursing had been a passion of mine, and I had always held onto hope that I would be able to return someday. Now, even that had been taken away from me. With my license gone, even the slightest possibility that I could repay Judge Speers's manufactured debt was completely extinguished.

In the months that followed, an investigator from the State Nursing Board contacted me. Several weeks later, I received legal paperwork from the State Board of Nursing. Within a few weeks, I received a phone call from the investigator to meet me at a fast food restaurant. "Bring your license; I'm taking it," he said.

Flying monkeys, or apaths, is a term used in popular psychology, mainly in the context of narcissistic abuse. They are people who act on behalf of a narcissist to a third party, usually for an abusive purpose such as a "smear campaign." The phrase has also been used to refer to people who act on behalf of a psychopath for a similar purpose. The term is not formally used in medical practice or teaching.

 "Abuse by proxy, or proxy abuse, is a closely related or synonymous concept. The term is from the flying monkeys used by the Wicked Witch of the West in the 1939 film Wizard of Oz to carry out evil deeds on her behalf." —Wikipedia

A Broken Heart

Well into the Fall, I started working on a motion for a change of venue for the child support case. I was hopeful that a new judge would be able to see what Judge Speer had done and free me from these charges.

One morning while I was working on the case, I was stopped in my tracks by a sharp, crushing pain that emanated from the right side of my chest. Soon, it had migrated to the left side, instead. I wasn't too worried about it, so I took three baby aspirin and a Clonopin to numb the pain. Fifteen minutes later, the pain was still there, so I called Brad at work and asked him what he thought I should do. "Call an ambulance!" he said, his voice on edge.

My pain wasn't unbearable by any means, so I was a little embarrassed about calling 911. The paramedics were at my door in less than ten minutes and brought a stretcher with them. "Could you turn the siren off?" I asked, looking around to see if any neighbors were watching, "And I don't need that stretcher. I can walk in myself."

The paramedics rejected my request. I got into the ambulance, and the paramedic placed an IV in my arm with excellent precision. He gave me a Nitroglycerin tablet, and we waited for five minutes to see if the pain would go away. It did not. I asked what my "P waves" were doing, a measurement that shows activity of the heart, but the paramedic wouldn't give me an answer. He gave me an IV with nothing but saline (saltwater) in it, and we headed to the hospital.

Once we arrived at the hospital, however, the nurses there were much more concerned. The nurse rushed in and started feeding me an IV of Nitroglycerin. They took my bloodwork and then the doctor came in. He listened to my heart and lungs and said, "Your respirations are at 41. That's not good. We are going to have to keep you."

"I really don't feel that bad," I said, "I think I'm okay, really. Besides, I have plans to go shopping tonight with Linda."

Linda, who was sitting in the room with me said, "Couldn't we do this on an outpatient basis?"

"No! Absolutely not," the doctor said.

The sharp, crushing pain in my chest was becoming unbearable, so the nurse increased my pain medicine dosage. The doctor returned and told me he was going to give me one milligram of Ativan to help me relax and ease the pain as well. It definitely helped.

"Our tests suggest that there is damage to your heart" The doctor said when he returned to the room. "We're not sure exactly what the cause is yet, but it might be Takostsubo, stress cardiomyopathy." Stress cardiomyopathy is a sudden, temporary weakening of the muscular portion of the heart caused by emotional stress, anxiety or a loss. It is commonly referred to as *Broken Heart Syndrome*. The Japanese term for broken heart syndrome is Takotsubo...how fitting!

"We're going to find a room on the heart floor to put you in," he said.

It was midnight when I arrived on the heart floor. My Troponin levels, an indication of heart damage, were still elevated, so the doctors decided to perform a heart catherization. I was shocked, and so were the doctors. I had perfect cholesterol and weighed only 130 pounds, so I was the last person that you'd expect to need heart surgery.

The next morning, I went down to the "Cath Lab." Friends and family, some that I hadn't seen in years, came to visit and support me. When I awoke from surgery, I was already in my room on the heart floor. Tina Craig was sitting in the corner of the room, smiling at me. "You did it!" she said. When I went into surgery, the Cardiologist took Tina to the back room to show her what they had found when working on my heart on a computerized screen. Tina told me that she came to the "Cath Lab" when all this was going on. There were three blockages to the left anterior descending artery. Tina told me he put in three stents, and that one had to go in a very small area because it was heavily blocked by plaque.

The Cardiologist came in while Tina was there, and told me that I would have to lay flat for about 6 hours. He further explained the procedure, and told me that if I hadn't been on Clonopin things could've been much worse. Soon after he left, Tina left too. I thanked her for coming and she said she would check on me tomorrow.

As soon as I returned home and could drive, I dropped off a doctor's letter regarding my heart attack and procedure to the courthouse.

Even my broken heart was not enough to convince Judge Speer that I was unable to pay child support. She rejected my cardiologist's note and insisted that I get a note of confirmation from my family physician instead. She refused to listen to my arguments because I was repeating myself, while she allowed Seth to repeat the same case over and over again for hours on end. How much more would Judge Speer take from me? Was she trying to give me another heart attack as well?

PART FIVE:
Lady Justice Arrives

A Superior Court
Case Goes My Way

I was laying on the couch, staring at the TV, when Brad brought in the mail. He threw a thick envelope onto my stomach. It was several days after Christmas, and I was having trouble focusing. All I could see were the ever-growing arrears mounting in my mind.

I held up the heavy envelope from the Superior Court. "Well, here's another case that's been affirmed," I said. When I started to peel open the envelope, however, my heart skipped a beat. The case had been vacated and remanded.

"Brad, come here!" I shouted. I gave him the form letter with tears of joy in my eyes. "We won! We won the child support case!" I said. His eyes grew wide and he embraced me.

Unfortunately, things weren't over yet, as the case had just been "remanded."

"What does that mean?" Brad asked. I told him that, had it been vacated, the arrears and everything would have been washed away. But since it was on remand, we had to go back to Judge Speer, and she would have to enter her own judgment, or lack thereof, on the ruling from Superior Court.

Still, it was a victory, and we had reason to celebrate. "Hold my hand!" I said to Brad, jumping onto the leather couch. Then I leapt off of it, laughing as I came to the ground. Long ago, I saw Tom Cruise do that on the Oprah Show, and I wanted to know what it felt like to be so happy that you could throw your whole self into it. I had finally won!

New Attorney, New Hope

For this case, I knew I couldn't risk representing myself as a Pro Se litigant. Despite my three-stent placement several months earlier, I was still having chest pain, and I had to avoid any unnecessary stress. I would have to find a new attorney.

I met with Attorney Cathryn L. Mills several weeks later. The first thing she said to me was, "Look, Judge Speer is really mad." After looking through my file, she told me, "I wish I would have met you over a year ago. You should never have gone to jail. That should not have happened."

Of course there was a blizzard on the day of my hearing. Why would anything go smoothly for me? My attorney was two-and-a-half hours away, and I worried that she wouldn't make it. She was already late. If she didn't make it, this hearing would have to wait for another day. Ten minutes later, my attorney arrived. I gave her a huge hug. Then, we approached the railing. As I stood at the railing, I found myself leaning on it and over it to hold myself up. I was exhausted from the stress of this and my heart attack and continued chest pain that warranted a re-catheterization to see if any new blockages had formed.

Judge Speer came out and the proceedings began. During the hearing, my attorney stated, "Your Honor, you can't have it both ways. You can't have someone who is being called mentally ill on top of having a heart attack and then expect them to work a full time job. Your Honor, you have to abide by what the Superior Court has ordered."

Judge Speer looked down at her paperwork, refusing to do so much as look at my attorney.

Whenever Attorney Black interrupted, my attorney would object, saying he was being argumentative. Judge Speer sustained all of my attorney's objections. It was amazing to watch. Attorney Black acknowledged my two wins at Superior Court and stated to Judge Speer, "She has an excellent track record at Superior Court."

After Judge Speer closed the arguments and left the bench, my attorney came over to me and said, "[Seth] makes over $100,000.00 a year!"

Walking out of there, Attorney Mills said, "I don't know how this will go, but it's clear to everyone that you are sick." She told me that she would keep in touch as the case continued.

When I received the order, I was overjoyed with the news. Judge Speer finally acknowledged that I no longer had the income capacity of a nurse. Judge Speer also ordered, "Ms. Petri's support shall be calculated in accordance with Ms. Petri's hourly wage of $7.25 an hour with her current job. Therefore, the defendant shall pay $110.00 a month for the support of three minor children."

Pension Fund Addressed

There still was the issue of the pension fund to address, which I still did not have access to. Judge Greene had ordered its release years ago at the beginning of this mess, but it had never occurred. In May, my attorney went before the Honorable Judge Kevin J. Franks., with Attorney Black in attendance, to discuss it. When my attorney questioned Attorney Black about this, he stumbled with his words and could never come up with a decent answer as to why the pension fund was not placed into the arrears that could have saved me from going to prison.

Judge Franks also asked Attorney Black over and over at length as to the multiple opportunities they had to get this down to Domestic Relations when it was ordered and now an attorney had to travel a distance to make sure this money got taken off the arrears.

Again, Attorney Black stumbled over his answers. I'm sure all that was planned out, too. I'm certain Attorney Black and Judge Greene just set it aside in order to cause me more legal fees and hardship.

Judge Greene's ruling, while he was still alive, was never entered into Domestic Relations for them to credit the arrears. It just never happened. This is a prime example of causing a defendant to rack up more attorney fees in order to get something done that was ordered months and months ago and, again, would have saved me from going to prison.

My attorney asked for attorney fees for traveling to the courthouse for something that should have been handled a long time ago. The Judge denied her request, however, he did leave open for any future litigation. Still, approximately $10,500 in arrears remained, arrears that never should have happened in the first place.

 # TAKEAWAY:

All this time, Seth had been cutting his income in half whenever he estimated it. Not only that, but when he took custody of my children, Domestic Relations gave him a downward deviation in his income because he had custody.

My children never reaped the benefits of his large salary. My sons could have had braces! My oldest son later told me, "Dad buys everything for my sister, and we have to work for everything." That was a classic sign of Seth grooming my daughter for Parental Alienation. He had started preying on her mind as early as the age of eight. He bought and used his own daughter; bought her everything just to keep her happy and away from me.

Seth's complaints of my being vexatious and litigious were completely false, as I was allowed to litigate in the manner that I had been per Connecticut law. He had told everyone that I was running him into the ground financially, when really, I was fighting for my life. For Seth to say that I was frivolously litigating in Superior Court just to be vexatious was a ridiculous statement at best. Had I not had that win with the child support, I know I would have been dead long ago; my death caused by a vindictive ex-husband, judge and a biased court system through the use of CPS that caused this mess on a whim of an almost seventeen-year-old not getting her way entwined with lies that destroyed my family beyond repair, especially my son's emotional wellbeing.

The fact remained that I had difficulty working even a menial job. The heart attack took its toll, the back issues, along with the migraines, anxiety, depression and PTSD were all I could deal with, which in turn, my husband had to handle. He had paid my attorney fees, jail fees, and child support and the arrearages for years after winning in Superior Court. If it was not for Brad helping me during this time, I don't know what I would have done; possibly end up in a women's shelter, never seeing my children again and/or back in prison. But we were warned by my previous attorney, that was their plan all along.

The Aftermath

It has been years since my time as a non-custodial parent, but the effects still remain on both myself and my children. Seth has never moved on, and has already turned two of my four children against me in his anger.

Looking back on my life with the information I have now, I can see the signs of the abuse Seth and Judith were exacting on my children. I only wish I could've seen it then. Even during the trials, my ex-husband read court transcripts aloud when my children came home from school, giving them blow-by-blow details of what happened as if it was a football game. They couldn't process all this information, which put them in an emotionally vulnerable state that allowed Seth to sow doubts into my children's heads about me. Then, when I was convicted and put into prison, Seth sat my children in front of a computer to see their beloved mother's mugshot; all for his own pleasure. My children's sweet memories of early childhood have been altered and replaced with lies created to destroy my relationship with them. All this is horrific emotional abuse that no child should experience.

Dr. Sol Goldstein, a child psychiatrist with four decades of experience in Parental Alienation calls it "the worst form of child abuse." He adds, "It's causing distortions in the mind and the distortions also work on the character, it alters the character of the child, so later on they have difficulties on every level of interpersonal relationships and personal thoughts about themselves. It's the most awful form of abuse and has to be recognized as such."

So why did no one recognize it in my children? The lawyers didn't see it and neither did the judge. CPS didn't even see it for what it was! Even the child psychologists had no idea what was actually playing out in the court room and were duped into believing Seth, who emotionally abused and neglected his children, all while feigning concern for their best interest.

There were many corrupt forces at play that allowed this to happen including whoever called CPS, and CPS for choosing to get involved where they didn't belong. That, along with a biased Family Court System with predetermined outcomes, inept psychologists that didn't understand Narcissistic Personality Disorders or Parental Alienation, a corrupt Judiciary System, and an unrealistic inflation of child support led to my eventual imprisonment. Family Laws and Protective Services are corrupted at every point.

Over the years, USA courts have learned to target fit parents instead of unfit parents because there isn't money to be made from the unfit ones. The parents who care about their child's wellbeing will do everything the courts demand of them to further their children's best interests. They are willing to pay hundreds of thousands of dollars for court supervisors and court officials and millions of dollars to attorneys. Even when these parents have evidence of abuse toward their children that occurred by the actions of the custodian guardian, the courts ignore their proof and discredit the fit parent until they have nothing left to give. Abusive or neglectful parents, if targeted, are likely to give in after the first hurdle.

Family and CPS court officials, evaluators, therapists, doctors, attorneys, court supervisors (for supervised visitations), Guardian

Ad Litems, and outside contract organizations (both for-profit and non-profit) all receive large weekly kickbacks from removing these children from safe and loving homes. There is a long list of those in each community.

I went into the court system naively hoping for truth and justice. I even believed that my ex-husband would be honest, thinking that he would want what was best for the children. Far from it. What I was exposed to, instead, and what many good parents are exposed to, was bias oppression, deceit and lies. It's almost as if you have walked under a hornet's nest and there's no getting away. These cases can drag on for years, as mine did. Unfortunately, there is no stopping the Family Court System. It's a money-making machine with judges recommending parents return to Family Court in a couple of months for either updates in their cases, continuous interviews.

Parents find out far too late that their case has been hopelessly mishandled, and this injustice keeps both parents coming, trying to fix the injustices that were done. In this broken system, Family Court allows Parental Alienation to thrive. They actually encourage parents to pit themselves against each other, causing anxiety, depression, hopelessness and helplessness to the point where some parents will even take their own lives, knowing that there will be no end to the corruption and financial burdens.

Unfortunately, there is little information available about how common this situation is. The reasons for this are manifold. In some cases, individual victims of the system may dismiss their experience as a bizarre set of circumstances. In other cases, gag orders are issued to the fit parent as soon as the child is placed with the unfit one and files are sealed from the public. Judges and caseworkers threaten the target-parent, saying that they will never see their children again if the gag orders are violated. This means that the fit parent is not allowed to speak to the media or seek support (i.e., from doctors, therapists, law enforcement, the media, or other outlets such as websites or blogs) on behalf of their child, children or themselves outside of the court's purview.

When the protective parent brings indisputable evidence against the abusive parent who has custody—such as photos, doctor's reports, taped conversations, and police reports—the protective parent can be prosecuted and thrown in jail on the grounds of Contempt of Court. Or even worse, their parental rights can be terminated. Not one of those reports can be used as evidence, unless the CPS caseworker or social workers agree to it. The Family and CPS Courts almost always defend their original decision even in the face of glaring evidence that the child suffers from severe neglect, physical torture, or sexual abuse, and they do it all for the money.

Keith Harmon Snow's book, *The Worst Interests of the Child: The Trafficking of Children and Parents through U.S. Family Courts*, states, "The violence and judicial abuse in Family Courts would not be possible without the support [corruption] of the Department of Children and Families [DHS/CPS]." Snow adds, "DCF ['CPS' is known under several names, depending on the State] provides one of the portals through which massive U.S. Department of Health and Human Services funding flows. As with the judicial abuse, there are no meaningful checks and balances on the DCF system and abuses are rampant." There are no regulations, and the CPS watchdog agency, the Ombudsman Agencies, has become equally corrupt. Quite simply, "The odds and prejudices are so heavily stacked against low-income families that trafficking children into foster homes is a multi-billion dollar business." Snow ends by saying, "It is no different from a hostage situation, knowing your child is in this level of organized danger. Parents are relentlessly terrorized by predatory court officials daily or weekly, for years, while hundreds of thousands of children in America are being needlessly abused, their lives permanently damaged."

Even when gag orders are not issued, many parents are scared silent. They fear that releasing damning evidence against the unfit parent could cause them to take their anger out on the children. They also fear retaliation from the courts. Other protective parents may be filled with shame and disbelief, thinking, "how could this have happened to me and my child when I did nothing wrong?" and "no one is going to believe me."

These loving, protective parents often cannot sleep at night after losing contact with their children, who now live with an abuser. They cannot protect them; they cannot help them, and they must live every night knowing that their child's wellbeing is completely out of their control. In almost all cases, they develop debilitating illnesses—gastrointestinal diseases and sometimes terminal cases of cancer because of the extreme stress. All of these consequences often leave the fit parent so sick and exasperated that they are unable to explain even to their friends, let alone the media, what has happened to them.

The victims who remain healthy are willing to sign away their homes and savings to the Family Court in order to secure the safety of their children. Family and CPS Courts extend the dispute over many years, typically over an entire decade, and protective parents give them everything, leaving them bankrupt financially and emotionally.

I cannot describe the horrible situation that abusive parents go through better than Edward Kruk did in his book, *The Life of the Alienated Parent, Coping with the Trauma of Parental Alienation* when he said, "As much as targeted parents desperately want to save their children, they cannot rescue their children; they cannot rescue them... from the quicksand by jumping into the quicksand with them. If they do, they will both perish. Instead, they must have their feet firmly planted on the ground, steady in your own emotional and psychological health, and then extend your hand to retrieve your child. But even then, given the nature of Parental Alienation and its profoundly damaging effects on a child, a child may not grasp the parent's hand."

Family and CPS Courts put on a twisted mask to hide their judicial abuses and private profiteering with phrases like "putting children first," or representing the "best interests of the child." It is not that far of a stretch to suggest the CPS and Family Courts' actions amount to racketeering and extortion. The Federal Courts could charge them with violations of the Racketeer Influenced and Corrupt Organizations (RICO) Act.

> *It's time to force CPS to acknowledge the crimes they have committed. They have failed to protect our children, and have instead caused the abuse, rape and death of hundreds of thousands of children across the country every year—not to mention the emotional and financial agony they have caused for their loving parents.*

Physical And Emotional Toll Of Legal Abuse

My family suffered the stress and duress of Legal Abuse for years. We have suffered from stomach ulcers, anxiety, depression and even a heart attack because of them. Was it all worth it? Of course it was, but it should not have come at such a high cost. Had I not won in Superior Court, I would be looking at going to prison every four or five months.

I was accused of being vexatious and litigious in court. Perhaps these accusations were justified. You would probably do the same thing if your children were ripped away from you, your career was destroyed and then you were thrown in prison all at the pleasure of a narcissistic abuser. But really, Seth was the one doing most of the litigation. I had to defend myself or die trying.

Legally, it was my right to file for the second custody trial. But after the subpoena of witnesses including my kids who wanted to go on the witness stand and have their say, only to have the event sabotaged before we even got there, was an extreme disappointment to all of us.

The win at Superior Court as a Pro Se litigant saved my life, but it was the corruption in the higher courts and in the lower courts that practically destroyed it, all at the hands of verbally abusive attorneys and judges who, with no grounds to back it up, accused me of being crazy. Once I could no longer afford an attorney, I was even more vulnerable.

Lady Justice Hidden

Maryann Petri

Lady Justice do you hide?
I seek the truth through you,
Your blindfold is thick yet shear
Are the lies hidden there too?

Why bother to hold the scales so proudly
When you dip your sword in bias,
Loss overwhelming with sadness
Swiftly judging innocents in defiance

Jurors and Defendants look to you
Judges and Lawyers are bought,
All hope in fairness is lost in a day
When Justice is all they had sought

How does Justice go on each day
Failing us all too many times,
On the whim of a corrupt judge
Bias was the player in the crimes

Epilogue

It was quite clear where Lady Justice stood. She stood at the watering holes of the elite and behind the closed doors in the Judge's Chambers and in the Family Law Courtrooms watching the judges and lawyers conspiring against you in your case, overseeing the dismantling of what was left of justice even before we walking into the courtroom. Lady Justice stood with her white gown flowing, holding the scales of so-called justice, ever so slightly tipping them one way while holding her sword at her side dripping with the blood of all the souls that suffered through Family Court, watching their families split apart and their beloved children torn away. Lady Justice frequented golf courses and social clubs where all the lawyers and judges discuss your case, coming to their own conclusions days prior to your hearing. Lady Justice watched, peeking under her blindfold, if she even wore one at all...

But the fight back was extremely well worth it. As a Pro Se litigant winning two cases out of three in the Superior Court, several attorneys have told me that's a good track record compared to any attorney. I knew I had to fight back, constantly reporting the injustices that flowed into my cases, and I will never stop fighting back. In fact, the fight continues.

The World Health Organization Recognizes Parental Alienation

Just recently, an article was written by Karen Woodall that the World Health Organization Recognizes *Parental Alienation.* "Despite the efforts of political ideological groups to prevent it, on May 25th 2019, the World Health Organization accepted the current version of ICD-11 which contains within it the index term Parental Alienation for the code QE.52 Caregiver-Child Relationship Problem.

The inclusion of Parental Alienation as the index term in ICD-11 comes after a long campaign led by Professor William Bernet, head of the Parental Alienation Study Group who has worked tirelessly to reach this day. Finally, the psychological manipulation of children of divorce and separation has the recognition generations of children have desperately needed us to achieve for them."

References

Keith Harmon Snow, *The Worst Interests of the Child: The Trafficking of Children and Parents through U.S. Family Courts* Burning Sage Publishing House

CTVNews.Ca

William Bernet, "Parental Alienation and the DSM V" *American Journal of Family Therapy* 38, 76-187, 2010

Dr. Craig Childress, Psy.D., *BeyondParentalAlienation.com*

Edward Kruk, Ph.D., "The Life of the Alienated Parent" *Psychology Today*, Nov. 5, 2017

Julio Rivera; *Townhall*, August 12, 2019

Barbara Fidler, Ph.D., C. Psych., ACC. FM.

Attorney Nick Bala, Queens University Law Professor

Dr, Mark D. Roseman, Divorce Coach and Consultant, Expert Witness for Child Custody Issues Specialties in Co-parenting, Parental Alienation and Family Court reform. Speaker and Trainer on Challenges for the Contemporary Child, Modern Family Matters, Parental Alienation. Writer and Researcher. Author of *Preserving Family Ties, An Authoritative Guide to Understanding Divorce and Child Custody*, Westbow Press, 2018.

Rod McCall, *For the Love of Eryk*, Triumph Press

Dr. Sol Goldstein, Child Psychologist from Toronto Canada

Dear Sophie, Facebook Page

Karen Woodall, "*WORLD HEALTH ORGANISATION RECOGNISES PARENTAL ALIENATION*," KarenWoodall. blog, May 27, 2019